Nobody's Child

The True Story of Growing up in a Yorkshire Children's Home

G.J. URQUHART

The History Press

For Robert, David, Moira, Jamie, Eleanor and Ivan,
with all my love.

First published 2020

The History Press
97 St George's Place,
Cheltenham, GL50 3QB
www.thehistorypress.co.uk

© G.J. Urquhart 2020

The right of G.J Urquhart to be identified as the Author
of this work has been asserted in accordance with the
Copyrights, Designs and Patents Act 1988.

British Library Cataloguing in Publication Data.
A catalogue record for this book is available from the British Library.

ISBN 978 0 7509 9508 5

Typesetting and origination by Typo•glyphix, Burton-on-Trent
Printed and bound in Britain by TJ Books Limited

CONTENTS

FOREWORD

Prior to the Second World War, orphans and other children who were lacking parental care frequently ended up in long-term residential care provided by charities or religious organisations. In addition, children who were destitute might find themselves in the care of county and borough councils who, in 1930, had taken over the responsibilities of the former workhouse authorities, together with their stock of institutional accommodation, much of which dated from Victorian times.

In 1945, the government appointed a committee, chaired by Miss Myra Curtis, to consider how best to make provision for children who, for whatever reason, were deprived of a normal home life or parental care. The committee's report recommended that for such children the best option was adoption, the next best being fostering, with institutional care the least favoured.

The report's proposals formed the basis of the 1948 Children Act, which gave local authorities the primary responsibility for providing care and supervision for any deprived child. To fulfil this broader remit, local authorities were required to appoint a Children's Committee and

Children's Officer to put the new approach into action. However, the limited supply of suitable adoptive and foster parents meant that residential care – often in rundown buildings – continued to play an important role.

It was into this fledgling system that three-year-old Gloria Urquhart was thrust in February 1950 when, after the loss of her mother, she was placed in the care of Leeds City Council's children's department. Her memoir provides a unique insider's view of this important, though rather neglected period when the modern-day care system was still finding its feet. Much more than this, though, her vivid and extraordinarily detailed memories of the people and places she encountered make compelling reading. Her life in the council's various homes veered between violent abuse and warmth and kindness, while a taste of life outside came via a weekend 'aunt and uncle' scheme, eventually leading to a long-term foster placement.

But at the heart of Gloria's chronicle is her determination to track down her birth family, especially her baby brother, Kevin – a journey whose twists and turns, joys and heartbreaks, battles with officials, and the ultimate triumph of her indomitable spirit – that makes this book so captivating and moving. When I first read Gloria's manuscript, I found it almost unputdownable. She is a wonderful writer and her story is one that will stay with you for a long time.

Peter Higginbotham
childrenshomes.org.uk

One

IDENTITY

'Your mother is dead and in a box with a lid on. You are not wanted!' shouted the woman who was stripping off my clothes.

I was so scared. If my mother was in a box, would a lid be put on this thing I was standing in? Would I soon be dead?

In reality, I had just been plunged into a large, white porcelain bath of hot soapy water and my hair covered with the foulest smelling cream, which quickly took away the terrible itching that made me scratch. I had never had a bath before. Whenever washing had been considered necessary, I was bodily lifted into the sink and scrubbed with a rough facecloth lathered with yellowish soap. Standing there in my birthday suit, I could look out over greying net curtains and watch other children playing in the street.

This new experience of a bath was so frightening. Crying was rewarded with hard slaps on my bare, wet legs that hurt terribly and left large red marks. Relieved to be physically pulled out of the bath still alive, I searched for my own clothes.

'They are in the dustbin!' yelled the woman. More tears, more slaps. I only wanted my own clothes! But I was forced to put on the ones provided. I was given a pair of black, ugly and very heavy shoes. I could not fasten the laces and was slapped again and told, 'You will soon learn.'

'Where are my own shoes with the buttons? I can fasten them,' I cried, as I tried desperately to tuck the leather laces into the shoes given to me. I stumbled down the stairs behind the awful woman.

Surely all would be well soon. After all, I had just left my father and my baby brother, Kevin in the hall downstairs. Despite the fact that Kevin had recently started to walk, he was on this occasion wrapped in a dirty shawl and firmly held in my father's arms. The woman who opened the door to us had told me to give Kevin a big cuddle and my daddy a kiss. I loved cuddling baby Kevin and had gladly held his tiny body against mine before being hauled off to the bathroom.

Returning to the hall, I was horrified to find no one there. I screamed and screamed as I realised I was now alone. I received such a beating from the woman who had bathed me. When the beatings ceased and I stopped crying, I was told, 'You are not wanted.' I could not understand what she was saying. Who didn't want me? The woman said, 'From now on you will live here with the other children.'

Broken hearted, I searched the building looking for my little brother and listened for his cry. All I could hear was the sound of lots of children's voices, who seemed to be coming from everywhere and were heading towards a room just off the hall. A very skinny girl with dark hair and broken teeth dragged me along to a huge dining room at the end of the long, musty smelling corridor. I was told to sit next to another girl, who dug me in my ribs and warned me in a brusque voice, 'Shut up and eat, or you will go to bed hungry.'

My salty tears trickled down into the corners of my mouth, adding some flavour to the otherwise bland food, which I was now forced to consume. That night, I slept fitfully in the strange bed, surrounded by the curled-up bodies of other girls who would wake in the morning and usher me along to the row of white stone handwash basins lining the ablution room wall. I was given a toothbrush and an enamelled pint pot already bearing a sticker with my name on. At least I had my own brush!

When it came to clothing, I joined the queue at the communal clothing store cupboard. After much searching, second-hand knickers, a liberty bodice and dress were hastily handed down to me. Again, I cried as I waited for the next instruction. An older girl took hold of my hand and gently squeezed it in a reassuring manner, which gave me a little comfort. I followed her into the dining room and began to eat the breakfast I was given.

I spent the rest of the day governed by a strict timetable and bellowed commands of dos and don'ts by the staff whose job it was to care for me. I was utterly scared in this alien environment. I could no longer play with other children in the street or run errands to the corner shop and be rewarded with a piece of bread and jam. I desperately longed to run away to my own home, but all the huge doors in my new abode were securely locked. So began my first day in the Reception Centre, Street Lane, Leeds, and the start of my life in children's homes.

★★★

Confusion reigned. Whatever had I done wrong? Only bad children are not wanted. My young mind could not decipher all the recent events. My father had gone. Kevin had been taken from me. I was alone in a very frightening place.

The deep anguish caused by the separation from my baby brother remained firmly rooted in my heart. His red hair, big blue eyes, lovely smile and a dirty shawl were my last memories of him. I held on to these brief memories in the deepest recesses of my mind.

The clothes provided by my mother and father had been thrown into a dustbin. I reasoned that if only I could find the bin, I could get my blue dress out of it and keep it, but the bins were outside the building, and I was locked in. I was two months off my fourth birthday, and at this age I probably had little concept of what condition my clothing was in. Even if other people thought my clothing unacceptable, they could be washed, and they were *my* clothes. Now, I had absolutely nothing to remind me of my former life with my family except a few memories and a deep longing to return home.

So traumatic were the events leading to the family breakdown and subsequent separation, followed by admission into this awful place, I could only think I was in some way to blame. A deep sense of rejection and inner loneliness lingered in my heart. There was no sign of Kevin anywhere. I grieved for the loss of the brotherly contact I had known. I was so sad and terribly lonely in this horrible, crowded place. I cried most of the time. I desperately wanted to return to my family.

Street Lane Reception Centre in Leeds was certainly not a pleasant environment for anyone to live in. I hated the awful musty smell of the entire building and found the long, dark corridors very scary. I longed to play out in the fresh air, but I was never allowed out of the building. I found the constant sound of children crying so distressing; their cries seemed to go unnoticed. There were no comforting arms, no cuddles and no love. The very tiny children seemed to spend hours sitting in long rows on metal potties. They were smacked hard if they tipped them and the contents over. Daily, I searched amongst the toddlers to see if I could find Kevin, but my search was in vain.

Whenever I saw the woman who had bathed me on my arrival, I was terribly afraid and bodily trembled. During the day, I remained in the dayroom along with other young children, who also seemed very frightened. There were no further beatings or aggression directed towards me. However, I did witness other distressed children being shouted at and sometimes beaten for what seemed very trivial reasons.

★★★

One day, a member of staff called out my name during breakfast. Nervously, I went with her to the staffroom. I was introduced to a very tall, thin woman by the name of Miss Goddard, who said she was my care worker. I had no idea what a care worker was.

'You are coming with me. There is someone I want you to see,' she said.

My heart pounded; I thought it might be Kevin. A taxi was parked outside the front door ready to take us to our destination. The driver left us at the bottom of a steep hill in an area of rundown houses. Many little children were playing in the street. Most looked dirty and dishevelled, but they were happy and running freely in their own back yards. I longingly watched them as I hurried along beside my first care worker.

'You are to accept the plans I have for you,' she said.

'What plans?' I asked myself. No one had told me anything.

We arrived at a very rough wooden door. Miss Goddard pushed it open. Stepping into the room, I was amazed to see an old lady lying in a bed near the window. I held back the tears of disappointment when I realised that it was not Kevin I had been brought to see. The lady must have been aware of my sadness and called me over to her side. She gently took my hand and said in a broad Yorkshire accent, 'I am sorry I can't take you, lass.'

Tears filled her old blue eyes and streamed down her wrinkled face. There followed a heated discussion between the two women. The old lady looked so ill and very sad. As we took our leave, she slid her hand under the little lacy cloth covering a small table near her bed and brought out a threepenny bit, which she placed in my hand. Reaching forward, she kissed my forehead with a rather toothless, sloppy kiss that I instantly rubbed away.

We returned to the main road where the taxi was waiting. Another adult and small child shared the taxi on our return journey to Street Lane. Not a single explanation was ever given to me about the day's events. All I could do was to hold on to the memory in the hope the future might throw some light on the visit. That same night, lying in the darkened dormitory as others around me slept, I sobbed until my whole body ached. I vowed I would one day find my little brother Kevin.

Two

ROTHWELL

Then came the day when I was bundled into a car along with some other children. No one had the grace or decency to explain to us that our destination was Rothwell Children's Home, Wood Lane, near Leeds. The old Victorian, red-brick buildings were known to the locals as 'The Orphanage', or to some folk as 'the bad kids' home'.

Despite the fact we had been bathed only a few hours before leaving the reception centre, on our arrival we were dunked in lukewarm soapy water and scrubbed around all orifices. Stinking of a second application of lice-killing disinfectant, we emerged, red-faced and aching into the laundry room. A bundle of clothing was handed to each child. An older girl insisted we get dressed quickly. We hastily redressed in the grey jumpers, black gymslips, horrible black stockings and shoes more suited to elephants' feet than our little feet. Only then did we realise we were not returning to Street Lane Reception Centre.

We had arrived at teatime. White pinafores were slung round our necks and draped over our second-hand attire. Entering one of the dining rooms, we were ushered to sit on hard wooden benches alongside long, scrubbed wooden tables almost identical to those in the reception centre. Other occupants joined us, and for what reason I cannot now recall, they began pelting us with eggshells and banana skins. As the youngest new arrival, I was scared. I did not enjoy my boiled egg.

After tea we watched the older children clear the tables and reset them for breakfast. Even the cornflakes were poured into the dishes. The next morning, the mice had left their droppings amongst the flakes. As newcomers, we watched in horror as the rest of the household flicked out the black specks and proceeded hungrily to devour their breakfast. I recall feeling quite sick at the thought of eating my breakfast but satisfying my hunger pangs soon blinded the eye to the black specks. The mice were frequent visitors to all areas around the orphanages; their numbers, I am sure, would easily match the 150 children in residence.

★★★

We were housed in one of four large red-brick buildings. A fifth building was used as a nursery. The sound of crying children constantly emanated from the nursery courtyard. On the outside of each building, a rusty wrought-iron staircase spiralled down to the ground from the third-floor landing. These ancient fire escapes were out of bounds to all but the staff. I was not sure if this meant we had to get permission to use it in the event of a fire! It seemed the mice required no one's permission; they frequently scampered up and down the steps, much to our amusement.

Around the front of the complex were large, black, wrought-iron railings and an enormous black gate where the so called 'good children' could peep through at the orphans, and we, on the other side, could stare back and put our tongues out at them. One of the older residents took me on a tour of the buildings. The entrance hall had a beautiful, patterned tile floor; all the colours and shining surfaces fascinated me. It would not be long before I would discover that hard work and sore knees would bring about the shine. A large, round, glazed pillar in the centre of the hall supported a rather old, crumbling ceiling. The walls were panelled in dark brown wood; some areas were scratched with names or drawings. I was told that anyone caught scratching the wall would get a severe beating. My informant added, 'Wait until your last day before scratching your name and then run like 'ell out of this place and don't come back.' I certainly felt like running like 'ell now!

On the ground floor, one room had lockers from floor to ceiling. I was assigned a low-level locker with my name on it. Inside was a wooden box for my outdoor shoes. Along the corridor, there were two more dining rooms, known to the children as the 'mouse holes' or 'Ratty's bedroom', due to the scampering of their feet across the stone floors.

The large kitchen was subdivided into two sections separated by a huge cooking range and numerous large, stone sinks. A group of boys were washing stacks of plates watched over by a stern-looking housemaster. I was warned there was always strict segregation in the kitchen area. We were never allowed to talk to the boys without the consent of our housemother. Girls were scrubbing pots and pans in a sink near the door. One girl was on her knees scrubbing the pantry floor. Turning to me, she said, 'I'll look after y'r, luv, when I've finished me scrubbing.'

True to her word, this girl, called Ellen, came and transferred my meagre possessions of a toothbrush and now an old, second-hand nightdress from the isolation room where the group of children from the reception centre had slept on the first night into a dormitory on the third floor. Sixteen girls slept here in very poor, cramped conditions. Each occupant had a small, black iron bedstead on top of which were neatly folded red or grey blankets, two sheets and a pillow.

I was assigned an old-looking wooden locker and shown how to fold items of clothing until they measured nine inches by nine, regardless of the bulkiness of some items. Thank goodness, I was the smallest in the room! As far as I could understand, the only garments that were stored here were vests, nightdresses and the black berets worn for church. Every other item of clothing seemed to come from the large linen cupboards outside the dormitory.

At the end of a long, cream-tiled corridor, there were two large bathrooms each with six deep, cast-iron baths and no screening between. On the floor beside the baths were wooden, slatted boards, known as duckboards. I was told these were scrubbed every Friday, hence the white and much-worn appearance. I was reminded that the signs of boys and girls only on the doors were to be strictly adhered to, on pain of punishment. Girls were forbidden to enter any part of the boys' sections of the building without a member of staff present. Recently introduced new rules allowed boys and girls to be together in the courtyard, but again only with staff in attendance. Ellen warned me that all broken house rules, and there were many, would result in a severe beating by the matron, Miss Silverwood.

★★★

So far, I had only met Miss Green, the senior member of our house, also known as the housemother, who treated me kindly. I soon discovered that Miss Green had a voice like a foghorn. When she shouted, we all jumped, but her voice belied her gentleness.

Our housemother had only one major dislike – nits in the hair – for which she had developed her own means of eradication. Every night before the little ones went to bed, they had to kneel down around the old fire range in the dining room, and while they sang hymns, the older children would tug fine toothcombs through each singer's hair. Any poor unwitting nit would soon wing its way into the roaring fire, and we would go to bed without the itch.

Each night, we sang a different hymn. One verse had to be learnt and sung solo by an individually named child. Older children were responsible for teaching younger children the words. One of the boys, who lived in the home opposite ours, was very musical and played the piano extremely well. He was allowed supervised visits to our house in order to teach us how to sing. He taught us the following words:

Now the day is over,
Night is drawing nigh,
Shadows of the evening,
Steal across the sky.

Now the darkness gathers,
Stars begin to peep,
Birds and bees and flowers,
Soon will be asleep.

When the morning wakens,
Then may I arise,
Pure and fresh and 'nit less'
In Thy holy eyes.

When my solo night came, I sang the last verse with great gusto, only to receive a sharp clip around the ear and a peal of laughter from the reverent kneelers. For punishment, both my errant instructor and I had to learn another verse:

Grant to every sufferer,
Watching late in pain,
Those who plan some evil,
From their heart restrain.

(Sabine Baring Gold, 1834–1924)

We also had to sing the correct words, 'Pure and fresh and sinless', ten times to ensure we would know the correct words in future.

Miss Green had a lovely singing voice and a good repertoire of classical, modern music and wartime songs. Our housemother often serenaded us with her rendering of Vera Lynn's 'White Cliffs of Dover' or Bing Crosby's latest ballads. We were encouraged to listen to the radio. I entered the imaginary world of the stories of the BBC Home

Service *Children's Hour*, a programme that came on about teatime. If you were in the house about four o'clock, you had to be quiet so the staff could listen to 'Mrs Dale's Diary'. Mrs Dale's family had a cat called Captain who, by all accounts, was well loved: we envied the cat!

Apart from these few minor likes and dislikes, Miss Green had very few restrictions. She treated each child with disciplined kindness. We heard from children in other blocks that their housemothers were always sending someone to Miss Silverwood, resulting in them getting very severe beatings and physical punishments. The only time we met the dreaded Matron was if Miss Green or other members of staff were on days off.

★★★

The cleanliness of our house was maintained by strict daily cleaning regimes set by the staff. Each day, a rota was pinned on the noticeboard, and every child, regardless of age or ability, had some chores to complete before nursery or school. How quickly I learned from the older children to complete any allocated chores and then hastily disappear behind the building – out of sight, out of mind!

We had to get up at six o'clock Monday to Friday and at seven at weekends. Our first task was to fold all bedding and stack it at the end of the bed. Windows were flung wide open, regardless of weather conditions, to air the beds. No bed bugs would survive the icy cold blasts that blew through the dormitories in winter! Bedroom floors were swept daily and scrubbed on Saturday mornings.

All dirty clothing was placed in wicker baskets, which were stored overnight at the end of each corridor. The next morning, two girls carried these heavy baskets down rickety flights of stairs, across a stone-flagged courtyard and into a huge laundry room that reeked of disinfectant that stung our eyes and irritated our noses. Older children on laundry duty would begin washing the endless items of clothing, ensuring all socks were placed into separate bowls for the younger children to wash by hand. Our fingers were often very raw and painful as we rubbed pink carbolic soap onto each sock, before dropping it into another bowl to be rinsed and squeezed through heavy old mangles and hung out to dry. In bad weather, the washing was draped over long wooden rods, suspended on large heavy pulleys, which required strong arms to hoist them up to ceiling height.

All these tasks had to be completed before the seven-thirty breakfast bell sounded, and a rush of hungry but exhausted children would walk in silence to the dining room. Breakfast dishes were washed in the deep stone sinks and restacked on shelves near the servery. Other items were re-laid, ready for the next meal.

As soon as these jobs were finished, those assigned to scrub the kitchen floor would begin their task. This was truly hard labour. It was difficult for the children to finish the floor with enough time to change into school uniforms and run as fast as their legs could carry them before the school bell would sound.

By the time the various tasks were completed, many children had little energy, and often less concentration levels, left. There were occasional reports of some children falling asleep at their desks. Often this led to the sleeper receiving punishments, both at school and in the home, and sometimes resulted in the allocation of harder tasks. This was horrendously cruel.

I was nearly five years old, still in the kindergarten and young enough to have a much-needed afternoon nap. I found this quiet time lying on a canvas cot covered by a grey blanket very peaceful, cosy and comforting. So far, I had not had to scrub the kitchen floor. I had, however, to scrub and polish the tiled hall floor along with older girls.

Most children, even those in dire circumstances, have the ability to turn work into fun. Amazingly, we found such moments in the general drudgery. The easiest way to clean the stair banister was to slide down it from top to bottom. If the staff had caught us enjoying our helter-skelter ride down the banister, we would have got a good hiding and possibly more punishing tasks to complete.

The tiled floors were scrubbed daily with hard scrubbing brushes. Ellen taught me how to wrap the floor cloth around the brush and wipe this across the floor, making the task less arduous. I was also shown how to drop the cloth into the bucket and use the brush if any staff came into the hall. One girl would be selected to act as a lookout and warn us of approaching staff.

We had great fun with the large, long-handled, heavy wooden bumpers used for polishing the floors. Liquid Ronuk polish was first spread over the floor and I soon learnt not to step on this slippery liquid after skating across it and landing heavily on my bottom. I laughed only because everyone else did, but I had a sore behind for several days. Beneath the blocks of wood, pieces of old woollen blankets were securely fastened with string.

An older girl showed me how to push the bumper with all my might to the girl opposite, who would return it in the same way. The floor would shine, and we developed large biceps, which could soon be put to good use if anyone thought of testing them at school. We sometimes held competitions to see which pair of girls could send the most bumpers flying. However, Ellen warned me not to be conned, as the winners were only doing more work than the rest! Little ones were easy targets for such a game.

★★★

Along the road from the orphanages there were several large buildings, known to the locals as the old workhouse, but posh, enlightened folk called it 'St George's Hospital'. Even in our time, it was a place to be dreaded. No one wanted to go there. We heard constant stories of people living in locked wards and never allowed out.

One day, I was taken along with some other girls into the first building; we were all terrified, fearing we too would be locked in forever. There seemed to be so many people moving about. Some had very strange expressions on their faces; others were mumbling odd sayings. One woman came over to me and started to stroke my face. She looked so old. Her face was wrinkled and care-worn; she had sad, deep brown eyes beneath white bushy eyebrows and thick whiskers on her chin. Her mousey colour hair had been plaited over her head.

She pursed her toothless mouth, pushing out her lips and pretended to throw me a kiss. I tried to move away from her, but she followed me. I moved again. Letting out a raucous laugh, she ran down the corridor and flopped down on a mat near the door. Another younger woman came towards me and grabbed the ribbon out of my hair. She pushed the bow under her lips like a moustache and started to waddle from side to side like a duck. I hastily covered my mouth in an attempt to stifle a giggle. Realising I would have to account for my lost ribbon, I reached out to retrieve it. A woman in crisp white uniform and brown-laced shoes grabbed hold of my coat collar and dragged me away. Releasing her hold on me, she ordered the group of now frightened children to march quickly behind her.

We hurried down a long, cream-tiled corridor and out under the glass-roofed walkway between two buildings, then out across a courtyard and into a small office. Here, we were ordered to undress. Our height was measured and charted on sheets of paper. We were asked to bend down and touch our toes, stand up and stretch our arms in the air and count to ten. The doctor asked each child if they had ever wet the bed and a large tick was scrawled across the page beside the offender's name. Children with ticks against their names were ordered to stand together and await a further medical examination.

I was in this large group, as I had unfortunately not developed full nocturnal bladder control. I certainly suffered the awful psychological pressure of a lecture every night about the badness of wetting the bed. I slept fitfully, fearing the wrath to come in the morning.

Daybreak always began with the shouts of the staff berating and humiliating the children who had failed to stay dry. If only they had realised all children have feelings and long-term memories! These harsh treatments only compounded the stress of not waking before the action of the bladder kicked in and, despite all attempts, we woke in a puddle of urine. Some staff even resorted to sending the poor wet child with sheets in hand to the matron's office for a beating for something that was certainly out with their control. We considered ourselves very fortunate if Miss Green was on morning duty. Her bellowing voice would wake us, but bed-wetters were treated more kindly. 'Go and get some clean sheets,' she would say, 'and ask God to forgive you.'

'Please God, forgive me for wetting the bed; I'm only little.'

We were all very relieved when the doctor instructed us to get dressed, and even more relieved when we returned to our usual accommodation. Although we hated living in the orphanages and longed to get away home to our families, we were very glad to be back on familiar ground and not left in the old workhouse.

Three

GRAVE HUNTING AND VISITORS

Sunday was always a more restful day. Only the minimal chores were done. For breakfast, we had boiled eggs and freshly made toast, with not a black speck in sight as the tables were wiped down before the toast was made. Weekday clothes were always stored away on Saturday night and Sunday-best clothes were issued for church. The floral dress I had been given was a few sizes too big, but I thought it was lovely, even though it was a little over-starched around the collar and left a red ring around my neck. The boys wore grey flannel suits, knee-length stockings and school caps that had never been to school! On cold, wet days, all children wore black gabardine raincoats over their attire. Only when coats were worn did we have to wear our obligatory black berets. How we hoped the sun would shine every Sunday!

Dressed in this manner, we would be marched in crocodile fashion, two by two, towards Rothwell village. The boys always led the way; their housemasters would bellow at any lad who broke ranks or turned around to look at the girls. The sad thing was that some of the boys had sisters in the care system, and they would try desperately to make contact with their siblings, only to be thrashed for their efforts if caught.

When pedestrians were coming towards us, we had to merge into single file and allow them to pass. Miss Green was a stickler for good manners, she would call out, 'Show respect and move over quickly!' However, many of the locals would pass us by on the opposite side of the road. Some of the children who saw this as rejection of the so-called 'bad kids', lived up to expectations and pulled gruesome faces behind their backs.

On arrival at the parish church, the boys would remove their caps. Everyone would gladly remove their itchy black woollen gloves, tuck one inside the other, and place them in a large box provided for our use just inside the door. A member of staff would give each child one penny. All 150 children plus staff would shake hands with the verger. The poor man must have dreaded our arrival, but his hand pains would soon be forgotten when he counted all the extra pennies in the collection plate!

Many of the children had lovely sweet musical voices, which resounded around the old stone building. At first, I joined in the singing too, if I knew the hymn. I could not understand why my singing prompted such stares from other children, until a young boy turned around and said, 'Shut up. Ya can't sing!' Thereafter, I mimed the words. (I may not have had a singing voice, but I could chatter. Many a surreptitious clip around my Yorkshire lug was aimed with such accuracy for my misdemeanours.)

Older and much wiser children had developed a sign language they used in the long sermons. In time, I too learnt their sign language, but there was no sign for giggling, so the clips around the ear kept coming.

As we waited for the crocodile line to form outside the church, I would look along the gravestones to see if any had my dead mother's name on it. Somehow, I had it in my mind that she may have had the same name as me, but there were none bearing my first name. At that stage in life, I could not spell my surname. However, that did not stop me from looking every week for her grave. Indeed, this became for me a Sunday ritual.

I made many an excuse that I needed to go to the outside toilet at the back of the church so I could look at the gravestones behind the building. On one of these jaunts, I came across some graves with bones and skulls carved on the stone. Back at the home, I asked what these graves were and was informed, 'Pirates that ull get ya.' I no longer needed the toilet, but this did not stop me hunting for my mother's grave at the front and side of the church.

★★★

Sunday lunch was always special. A large roast of beef was carved on the kitchen table and served with Yorkshire pudding, gravy, over-stewed cabbage or mushy peas. Again, manners were important. Miss Green insisted we wait until everyone had been served and grace said before we could start eating. Many a scrap of food found its way into hungry mouths during grace. We would peep out and ensure Miss Green's eyes were reverently closed. Of course, they were always firmly shut!

After lunch, we were sent out into the playing fields behind the home, regardless of weather conditions. At one end of the field, a large wooden hut provided shelter in bad weather. Inside, children sometimes used the raised wooden stage to enact their life stories. On other occasions, there would be rehearsals for seasonal fundraising concerts and plays for the village 'good kids' and their parents. Most children preferred to play out of doors, however.

There were strict rules for Sundays. Surprisingly, we could use the swings, but only if we did not rattle the chains loudly. Singing in the yard was banned for fear of disturbing the neighbours. Ball games and skipping ropes were not allowed. I could not understand why we could do all these things come Monday without fear of reprisal. Perhaps our neighbours only enjoyed the cacophony of children's voices on weekdays!

Some of the girls showed me how the seedpods of the willow herb plant, which grew profusely in the grounds around the home, could be split open revealing long silky threads. Together, we collected the pods and planned the day when we would have enough to make silk dresses. We were most disappointed when our first collection turned into dry shrivelled seeds that we scattered with our dreams.

Sometimes, staff organised competitions between the different houses. Often both boys and girls would make daisy chains to see who could create the longest chain without snapping it. We then gave our chain to someone else as a token of our friendship. I always felt very proud if someone gave me his or her chain to wear. If a handsome boy presented you with his chain and you blushed with pride, there would be moments of hilarity. If the chain broke as it was placed around your neck, you were supposed to kiss the giver and accept their forgiveness. Usually, the boys chose not to be forgiven and ran away, perhaps knowing that if staff saw them kissing a girl, a beating would follow.

The swings at the back of the buildings were in regular use by all age groups. I began to enjoy the swings and would often swing so high that the chains would shake violently. From this height, I could see over the wall into the back yards of neighbouring houses. I would strain my eyes looking to see if I could see any babies. In my mind, I had left Kevin in the world outside this orphanage. I was willing to risk the swing chains rattling in my attempt to find my little brother. Older, taller children knew areas where they could climb the walls and look over. I knew this could result in severe beatings from Miss Silverwood for anyone caught in the act. I never ventured near the wall, preferring my antics on the swings.

I was, however, brave enough to go to the nursery section and peep through the windows. There were many large prams in the hall; each one had a brown label attached to the handle on which was printed a name. I was too far away to see if Kevin's name was there. One day, a member of staff saw me peeping through the window. I made a hasty retreat. I hid behind some large dustbins before the big door opened and an irate nursery nurse gave chase in the wrong direction, much to my amusement. I was expecting to be hauled out of the dining room at the next mealtime and reprimanded by Miss Green for my misdemeanour, but it soon became apparent that the nurse had not reported me. Perhaps she did not know my name. It was not uncommon for some staff to be unaware of a child's name. With so many children in the orphanage, and constant changes, even the most astute person would have difficulty remembering every child by name. I was at the time usually referred to as 'GJ'. It was a very common practice to change children's names in the homes; perhaps this was to alter the identity of some children to prevent parents from tracing their whereabouts.

★★★

One day, while enjoying a session on the swings, I was stopped by a member of staff and taken to the recreation hut. Visitors had come to see me.

Sitting on the edge of the stage was a small man. I could see dark hairs poking out from his opened shirt collar. This really fascinated me and was the only physical detail I could later recall. He introduced me to the woman sitting beside him as 'Auntie Irene'. I had no idea who they were. For some reason, I did not recognise the man's face or remember what he was wearing; neither did I take any real interest in the woman, and the word 'auntie' meant nothing to me. After all, we had to call all female visitors 'auntie'.

No one told me who the visitors were until after they had left. One of the older children told me she had overheard a member of staff say it was my father and his new woman. Confusion reigned again. How could I have forgotten what my father looked like, and who was this woman? Why did they not take me home? If only I had known who the people were, I could have asked where baby Kevin was. Tears flowed. I vented my frustration on the swings as I rattled the chains even harder.

On two occasions, people I had never known before asked to see me. They looked at me and asked various questions. One couple took me out for the day, but I was soon told I was not wanted by them. Perhaps they didn't like my auburn hair!

Another couple came and looked at me. They indicated they were not interested when asked if they wanted to take me out. Other children had similar experiences. We all craved to live in 'normal' homes and be cared for with kindness, and above all loved, but we detested the way we were being viewed by these strangers. We referred to these visits as 'penny peep shows' and hated the rejection that ensued. There was no doubt that as children we felt very keenly the added stress of being treated like objects, and more often than not, rejected.

Younger children had to rely on the older, wiser housemates to tell us we were up for fostering with a view to later adoption. With very little understanding of what adoption meant, we could only listen to those who had returned from houses in the big outside world.

Some children literally disappeared with the foster families and we never saw them again. We could only hope they had found happiness. However, other children had passed through the initial fostering system, and for various reasons returned to the homes. I could not understand why they vowed they would rather stay where they were – until they recounted their experiences.

I was shocked when I heard how badly some of the children had been treated. Until now, I had imagined that all 'real family homes' were happy places of love, gentleness and kindness. Several children told stories of very poor living conditions, severe beatings and excessive housework. Others spoke of lack of food, and harsher conditions than we were coping with in Rothwell. A few children had better experiences, and desperately wanted the opportunity to stay with the families who had taken them on trial visits. However, they had been returned into care without any verbal reason given as to why they had been classed as unsuitable and therefore rejected. These events certainly made me feel terribly anxious. I, too, joined the ranks of disappointed children.

★★★

It was so amazing how some of the older children took it upon themselves to put their arms around a returned, sad child to comfort them. However, not all of the returned children cried. Many expressed their disappointment in the form of real anger and thought little of venting this on the younger housemates. I soon learnt to keep out of their way.

The tremendous psychological pressure put upon very young shoulders, and the stress manifested by the distraught children took on various behaviour patterns. Some children rocked quite violently on their beds; others used to bang their heads on walls or furniture. I saw one girl literally pull her hair out until she was quite bald. Another child, about eight years old, tried to cut herself with the cutlery in the kitchen. She was then barred from kitchen duties – instead, she was forced to dig the garden in all weathers.

Only when the lights were out at night did we share our thoughts and fears with trusted roommates. We tried to comfort each other, but inwardly we were all utterly confused and very lonely. The darkened dormitory became so symbolic of the deep-seated and fearful thoughts of all of us who experienced further situations of rejection. Despite the fears, most children still longed for someone to come and take them into a real loving and caring family setting. I longed for a good home.

I was beginning to piece together some facts. I knew I had a brother called Kevin, and now I was aware of my father's visit. These two details made me question how, if I belonged to these two people, could I be branded an orphan? I had been told that orphans had nobody to call their own. If I was not an orphan, why was I in an orphanage?

I asked one of the older girls if she was a real orphan and was surprised when she told me she had three older brothers. Sitting together cross-legged on the flagstones near the kitchen door, I listened to her account of a beautiful summer's day when she had been out walking with her mother. Together, as they crossed the road, a passing car had ploughed into her mother, pinning her against a wall. She later died of her injuries. Her mother had been the only breadwinner. Her father suffered badly from war wounds and, despite his love for his children, he was unable to work and support them. Now, all four children were in separate children's homes. Here was a loving, but divided family.

Hearing this story, I realised that not all children in care are there through parental neglect or rejection. If only I could turn back the clock. I could ask the man (if it was my father who had just visited me) why he had left me in hands of Miss Silverwood and her assistants.

Four

MICHAEL

I awoke one morning to hear the girls in my dormitory singing 'Happy birthday to you'. Several girls came and gave me a hug. However, my birthday came and went without any further celebration.

Birthday parties were things we heard other people talk about, but never experienced in the orphanage. Now five years old, I had transferred from the Monday to Thursday warmth and security of kindergarten to a full week at Rothwell Haigh Primary School. Like many little children, I was very anxious when my carer left me at the school gates and told me to make my own way into school. I entered the building with her harsh words ringing in my ear, 'When the home time bell rings, you get y'r sel back here as quick as y'r legs ull carry y'r as y'r on dining room rota.'

Tearfully, I watched mothers gently encouraging their little children into the building with hugs and kisses and loving words of reassurance. I felt so bereft of love. I was told at breakfast time that all children had to attend school, and for at least ten years.

In fear and trepidation, I stepped into the maze of school corridors and classrooms. I followed the crowd into the cloakroom and hung my black gabardine coat on the first hook by the door. An older girl removed it and hung it on a hook with a picture of a dog above it, saying, 'This is your hook. Come with me, and I'll show you your classroom.' Obediently, I followed her into a large room full of wooden benches and well-scratched desks.

My first teacher was middle-aged, but very energetic. After morning assembly, our class danced around the gymnasium, skipped through hoops and threw beanbags in the air. If we were clever enough, we caught them, much to our teacher's praise. We spent the afternoon rolling out and cutting balls of Plasticine (modelling clay) into halves, then quarters, without much mathematical precision. We were learning through play.

School opened new doors for me, doors behind which I could be a child, not a slave to rigorous cleaning regimes. Here, I was free to explore new horizons, gain knowledge and make new friends. I was disappointed when the bell signalled that it was time for the younger children to go home. I enviously watched as parents cuddled and kissed their little ones. Tears streamed down my face as I hurried alone along the road to the orphanage. In the days to come, I realised that none of the staff from the orphanage would attend concerts or sports days held at the school. Such events highlighted our lack of real parental care. Gradually, I looked forward to the start of the school week.

★★★

One morning, I was horrified on waking when a member of staff instructed me to wear my Sunday dress. I thought I must be going to the church. I protested and reminded her that this was Monday. 'Don't be so cheeky. Just do as I say,' she said as she left the room, leaving me standing there so bewildered.

My carer returned and ushered me into a waiting taxi. I was amazed and rather anxious when we arrived at the door of Street Lane Children's Home Reception Centre. Some of the staff came and spoke to me. There was only one person I recognised. 'My goodness, how you have grown,' she said as she adjusted the ribbon in my hair.

We crossed the yard and entered another house that was used as a nursery. Here, children between the ages of one to four years were gathered; many were tearful, but the staff did not respond to their cries. Large prams were lined up against open windows. Crying babies lay uncovered, having kicked off their blankets. I desperately wanted to lift one up and cuddle it close to me, just as I used to when Kevin cried, but my carer grabbed me by the arm and took me into another room. I remembered so well the smell of wet nappies and the stained carpets.

I was introduced to one little child. I stood and stared at this little boy. He had bright red hair and lovely big blue eyes. I thought he was Kevin. My heart sank when the woman with him said, 'This is Michael.' For a brief moment, I thought I had found my long-lost brother. On the journey to Street Lane, I had been given a very small bar of Cadbury's chocolate. When the little boy saw the chocolate, he grabbed the piece I offered him and ran away and ate it before returning and taking the rest of the bar out of my hand. He ran away again into a corner. He consumed the chocolate with such speed, I thought he must be very hungry. I was hastily removed from his presence. On our return journey, I asked who the little boy was and received the reply, 'He's just one of the kids in the nursery'.

Lying in bed that same night, I related the events to my roommates. The suggestion was put to me that the little boy might have been Kevin, now known by another name, Michael. I could not visualise Kevin as a boy. I only had memories of a little baby with red hair, big blue eyes and a dirty shawl. Suddenly, it dawned on me: if I was now five, Kevin must be about three years old. Terribly confused, I cried myself to sleep again.

Any questions to the staff about this visit brought a wall of silence. Even when I asked Miss Green, our housemother, who this little boy was, she took hold of my hand, held it firmly but gently in hers and told me to forget about the visit. Having received no explanation about the day's events, I remained baffled and greatly distressed. Again, I mentally stored the picture of this little boy and his love of chocolate away in my mind.

★★★

Now I had two very clear memories and two different names I could associate with Kevin. I also had a very heavy heart. I had failed again to trace him and look after him. For many days, I cried when alone. I could not concentrate on lessons at school, and this prompted punishment for my inattention. Standing in the corner of the classroom with my hands on my head only heightened my sense of failure and increased a deep sense of humiliation. To me, it seemed the adults were building a wall of silence around my inquisitive mind. All questions regarding my own family remained unanswered.

One member of staff told me to 'wipe that sulk off your face'. I slid my forearm across my face, only to receive a sharp slap from her. I was too young to fully understand my feelings, let alone share them with adults who had no answers to offer. My deep desire to belong to somebody seemed insurmountable. Even my primary school teacher, who to date had been very caring towards me, had also joined the silent ranks. During school time, I held back the tears. I wondered if Kevin knew he had a sister.

I was not the only child to cry at night. I now shared a dormitory with sixteen older girls; some of them could relate details of how their brothers and sisters had disappeared on the day they were brought to Rothwell. Other children told horrendous stories of separations from parents and a few recalled literally being dragged away from their families with no explanation as to why this was necessary, and all thought they must have been to blame.

Most of the younger children's memories, before entering the care system, were like mine – fragmented. Although we were barred from knowing our histories, we were not shielded from the sights of abused and neglected children being admitted into Rothwell. The most distressing sights were children who arrived dressed in rags, having been literally starved of food and shelter. We called these children 'waifs and strays'. I saw one child whose ribcage was showing through his skin, and I could count the bones. He screamed all the way to the boys' quarters.

There were times, although rare, when parents came to the gates, snatched their children and tried to escape with them. The poor children were then snatched back by social workers and hastily transferred to other homes. I used to wonder why parents allowed these events to take place, but no one could answer my questions.

Sometimes, children's names were called out at breakfast time. We knew these children would not be going to school that day. On our return from school, we would find our friends had literally disappeared from our lives. Rumours of fostering and adoptions would abound, and even children shipped across the sea to foreign places, but the staff always remained tight-lipped. No one knew from day to day who would be taken away, or who would be left in this awful place.

Five

A NEW WORLD
OUTSIDE THE WALLS

One cold winter's day, I was told to go over to the hut along with some younger children. I thought we were being allowed extra playtime. I was thrilled when I saw the hut was still decorated with the lovely coloured paper Christmas streamers we had spent hours making. Christmas Day had been extra special for us. We had all received a present from under the tree and another from Santa Claus, who came on a sleigh, but looked like the vicar of Holy Trinity Church in Rothwell village. After tea, we had played games before some of the children put on a nativity play. I loved the story of baby Jesus but was disappointed I was not chosen to play Mary, his mother.

I was standing by the lovely big Christmas tree admiring all the coloured baubles when two people came towards me. I disappeared round the back of the tree and peeped between the branches at the man who was trying to peep through at me. He smiled, and so did I. He changed my shyness into a game of hide-and-seek. For a few moments, we played this game together until I left my tree cover and came out into the open.

I was introduced to a lady who was wearing beautiful clothes, had lovely snowy white hair, blue eyes and a gentle voice. The man was not quite as tall as the lady. Around his neck he wore a white dog collar like the local vicar. I was told this person was known as 'the minister', which I understood was another name for a vicar. So, I put out my hand for him to shake it – I was used to shaking vicars' hands!

We left the hut and entered the main building where the visitors were offered a seat in the hall. Suddenly, without warning, I was whisked away to the bathroom by Miss Green. I was stripped of all clothing, then scrubbed with such haste and redressed in clean underwear and my Sunday floral dress, even though this was Saturday! A blue ribbon was tied in my hair. My hated beret was carefully angled on my head so as not to dislodge the bow. I was given a coat I had never seen before and told to fasten it quickly and put on the gloves now provided. Miss Green hurried me down the two flights of stairs into the hall where the beautiful lady was sitting next to my new-found friend.

I was a little uncertain when the two new people in my life took me out of the front gates and on to the bus. Perhaps some of the uncertainty stemmed from the stories I had heard in the dormitories from those who been taken out by strangers. We arrived in Leeds, a big city I had no previous recollection of seeing before. I was taken to a huge shop in the town (later in life I was to know this shop as Schofields, a high-class shop in the Headrow, in Leeds).

This large department store seemed so wonderful, especially when we arrived at the children's department. Hanging on white wooden coat hangers were beautiful little girls' dresses. I was asked which one I would like to try on. I chose a blue dress with a little white lace collar and was most disappointed when I had to take it off again. Other items of clothing were chosen for me. The shop assistant neatly folded all the new clothes and carefully wrapped the blue dress in white tissue paper and placed it in a large carrier bag, much to my delight.

We made our way to the restaurant. A waitress wearing a black dress and white frilly apron showed us to our seats. I was quite mesmerised by the crispness of the white, starched tablecloths, and could not believe that such beautifully laid tables existed; I had only ever seen the scrubbed wooden tables in the orphanage. Another server brought some sandwiches and the most delicious cream cakes I had ever seen on a three-tier cake stand. The tea was poured from a shiny silver teapot into the china cups through a little strainer. I was fascinated to see how the tea leaves stayed in the strainer and did not fall into the cup.

This was so different from tea served in the homes, where the leaves clung to the bottom and sides of the enamelled mugs. Some of the girls who were of Romany stock would read your leaves and tell you about good or bad things that awaited you in the future. Had Miss Green caught us scanning the bottoms of our mugs, she would have frowned on such practices. Secretly, I hoped these new tea leaves meant many happy times ahead.

Knowing I was never allowed to eat before grace had been said, I put my hands together and half closed my eyes so I could keep an eye on the cake I wanted. The minister asked me to repeat after him:

Thank you for the world so sweet,

Thank you for the food we eat,

Thank you for the birds that sing,

Thank you, God, for everything. Amen.

A white napkin was carefully tucked into the collar of my dress. How disappointed I was when I discovered that I had to eat some sandwiches off the bottom plate before taking the cake of my choice from the top of the cake stand. I so enjoyed this newfound freedom to choose my own food and not have to eat the same as everybody else. However, I soon found my eyes were bigger than my tummy. I could eat no more and thanked the lady and gentleman for my tea. I was desperately trying to be good, so I would be allowed to keep the pretty dress that was still in the big bag.

The minister and his wife asked me if I would like to stay with them until the next day. Although I was very apprehensive, I said, 'Yes please.'

I wondered if the good manners taught by Miss Green had impressed
my new benefactors.

★★★

The long journey on the tram was another new experience. Standing
at the front of the carriage with my nose pressed hard against the glass,
I watched the driver operating the big brass handle that made the tram
trundle along the tracks. On reaching our destination, Beeston Hill, the
man wearing the dog collar lifted me up so I could pull the cord to ring
the bell. The smartly dressed driver turned around and smiled at me as
he applied the brakes.

There were many streets criss-crossing each other, all with rows of
identical-looking, red-bricked terraced houses. We finally arrived at
Cranbrook Avenue. The house, I was told, was known as 'the manse', as
it belonged to the Church. The name sounded so good, far better than
the 'bad kids' home'.

The inside of this home was lovely and warm, not at all like the
draughty and very cold orphanage. The hall was so tiny. There was no
locker room where I could put my outdoor clothes. Instead, the lady
hung them on the wooden stand near the door. The fireplace in the
front room was so different from the huge black range I had polished
so often in Rothwell. This one was small, its two doors opened to reveal
the lovely coloured flames, flickering up the chimney. The man went to
the fire and poked the coals with a long-handled poker, sending even
more heat out into the room.

In the centre of the room stood a large brass coffee table with
wooden twisted legs. I ran my fingers up and down the spirals. The lady
with the blue eyes said, 'The table was especially made for me when I
lived in China.' I had no idea where China was. Placed on the table was
a glass of milk for me, but I was too excited to drink it.

A large bookcase lined the whole of one wall. I had never seen so
many books before. Near the bookcase stood a large roll-top desk. I
was intrigued that when the man opened the desk lid, the top

disappeared, only to return when the desk was closed. I was gently but firmly warned not to put my hands under the lid and was asked to refrain from touching the contents inside without permission.

At the back of the house there was a small dining room. Around a highly polished table were six rather ornate-looking chairs. From here, I had to step down into the kitchen. The pots and pans laid out neatly along paper-lace-edged shelves were a fraction of the size of those we had in the orphanage. The tiny brown stone sink in the corner was empty. There were no mountains of dishes to wash. I reasoned that, even if this kitchen floor had to be scrubbed, it was so small it would only take me a few minutes.

The lady offered me some grapes. I had never seen grapes before, let alone tasted them. I took one and sucked hard until the juice oozed into my mouth; they were so delicious. I really didn't want to hand them round, but Miss Green's training to always share even what little we had prompted me to reluctantly offer up the dish to the minister, who politely took a grape and gently popped it into my mouth, instead of his mouth. I felt a surge of happiness pass through me.

I enquired where I was going to sleep. The bedroom bore no resemblance to the sixteen-bedded dormitory in the orphanage. Here, there were only two beds, separated by a little cupboard with a lamp on top; its light cast a lovely warm glow around the room. Both beds were covered with beautiful, deep blue silky eiderdowns. At bedtime, instead of kneeling around the old black fire range and listening to staff bellow out instructions to pray for forgiveness – for what, I never knew – the lady and gentleman knelt down quietly beside the bed. I knelt between them and said my prayers. I remembered to thank God for this lovely home. I asked God if Kevin could come and live in this lovely home, too.

The minister said, 'Who is Kevin?'

I quickly replied, 'He is my baby brother who is now lost, and I want to find him. Will you help me?'

The minister just smiled.

Instead of having the harsh toothcomb dragged through my hair, it was very gently brushed with a real silver-backed hairbrush.

I was soon tucked up cosily in my new bed. I was lovingly kissed, cuddled and wished a good night's rest. The lady asked me if I would like to call her Auntie Marjorie, and the minister, Uncle William. So ended my first day with Marjorie and William Legassick.

For the first time in my short life, I was so happy and contented. The little lamp on the bedside table was left on for me. This was my first recollection of sleeping in a bedroom on my own and in a real home. I could not believe how quiet the house was; there was no drone of human voices, as would be heard in the orphanage. I had never been in an environment of such peace and tranquillity before. Surprisingly, I found it most comforting. I hoped I would be able to stay here forever.

Left alone, I got up and peeped around a curtain hanging across a small recess in the corner of the room. There were lots of ladies' dresses and coats. At the end of the metal rail hung my new blue dress, on a lacy-covered coat hanger. Contented knowing it was there, I jumped back into bed. Feelings of sheer delight passed through my whole being. Tears of joy streamed down my face. I rubbed them away on the white-frilled pillowcase and snuggled down under the silky blue eiderdown.

Six

MANSE CHILD

As usual, I woke at about six o'clock, fully expecting to hear the staff bellowing, 'Get up, and get up!' This house seemed so peaceful and quiet. Climbing out of my new comfortable dry bed, I went over to the window and peeped out from behind the heavy floral curtains.

My bedroom was at the back of the house and overlooked a small back yard. There was one tree gently swaying in the breeze. Birds were already eating scraps of food from a wooden bird table. Beyond the green-painted wooden gate, a narrow road separated one row of houses from the next. All the red-brick houses looked alike; even the chimney pots were the same. Only the net curtains were different. The house directly opposite had some very pretty white lace ones, and the one next door had heavier cream-netted drapes.

I wanted to use the bathroom. However, afraid I might venture into the wrong room, I stood cross-legged at the window enjoying the tranquillity. My thoughts were interrupted as the bedroom door opened, and in came my new friend. In a very soft voice, the lady asked me, 'Did you sleep well, darling?'

I loved the sound of her voice; it was so gentle. I told her I had slept well, and I had decided I would call her 'Auntie' because I liked her blue eiderdown. This story of my acceptance of Auntie Marjorie would be retold to so many people. For now, my childlike innocence made my new auntie laugh. Uncle William joined us. He gave me such a warm tender cuddle. I could never remember feeling so at ease with anyone else. It was such a great thrill to be allowed to come downstairs, wearing a soft pink dressing gown and slippers of the same colour.

***

Breakfast was served in the dining room. The little white napkin was removed from its silver ring and tucked around my neck. The cereal was poured into delicate china bowls. In this house, there were no awful enamel dishes and mugs and no mice droppings. There was no separate staff table here; we all sat together and used the same delicate china dishes and real silver cutlery. I loved the lacy tablecloth with its embroidered flowers in soft pastel shades on each corner. My new auntie explained how her mother had made the cloth especially for their wedding gift only a few years ago. It was so beautiful. I asked if she would be able to teach me how to sew when I grew up.

Uncle William taught me a new grace: 'For what we are about to receive, may the Lord make us truly thankful. Amen.' I liked this grace; it was very short, and I could eat my chosen cereal, toast and honey. At the end of the meal, I asked to see the work rota. I was more than delighted when Auntie Marjorie said, 'We do not have a rota in this house, darling. We are all expected to help one another.' I happily picked up the tea towel and rather anxiously dried the fragile dishes. There was no floor to scrub!

I was taken upstairs and dressed in my brand-new underwear and the lovely blue dress. The materials were soft and delicate against my skin, so unlike the hard, starched clothing I usually wore in the orphanage. I felt very special as I walked down the steep hill towards the church with Auntie Marjorie. I had never worn such lovely clothes before. Imagine my joy when I was told they were mine to keep. This was the first time since my admission to the care system, when my parents' choice of clothing had been thrown into the dustbin, that I actually owned my own clothes.

A rather plump woman and young boy joined us as we walked to church. I was introduced to Mrs Wilson and her son, Alan. I instantly liked Alan. He was a little younger than I was, but about the same height. He chatted away to me as though we had been friends for a very long time. His father, a deacon of the church, greeted us at the church door. Shaking my hand, he said, 'Alan will look after you and show you where to go for the Sunday school.' There seemed to be such a lot of people shaking hands with Auntie Marjorie. My hand was well shaken, and my pretty dress admired.

When the organ stopped playing, I was so amazed to see Uncle come though the vestry door. He was wearing what looked like a black cloak with a hood on the back. He climbed the pulpit steps and began to tell everyone my name and welcomed me into the congregation. Suddenly, I felt very shy and wanted to leave. I was sitting between Auntie Marjorie and another person who told me her name was Agnes, so there was no escape.

After the singing of a few hymns, Uncle William told the children a story, before Alan, who had been sitting behind us with his parents, came to the end of the row and beckoned me to go with him. Nervously, I followed him into the Sunday school room at the back of the building. When the teachers began telling us more stories about Jesus and his goodness, I soon forgot my fears and enjoyed being with the other children.

Returning to the manse after the service, Uncle William asked me what stories I had heard and which one I had enjoyed. I cannot now recall which story I related, but I do recall the hymn I liked and asked if he could sing it to me, and so he sang:

There is a green hill far away,
Without a city wall,
Where the dear Lord was crucified,
Who died to save us all.

I asked what 'crucified' meant and was told it was how Jesus died. I wanted to know if this was how my mother had died, but it seemed no one wanted to answer my question. For now, I forgot about it.

★★★

In the afternoon, several other families joined us. Together, we went for a walk in Crossflatts Park: its boundary bordered on Cranbrook Avenue. We were not allowed to play on the swings as this was Sunday. I did wonder why orphans in Rothwell were allowed to swing to their hearts' content on Sundays (although ball games were banned), but here swings were forbidden. However, when I saw how little the swings were in comparison to the high swings I was already used to, I soon forgot my disappointment.

I enjoyed seeing all the beautiful flowerbeds and encouraged by Auntie Marjorie to smell the roses, I was amazed at the fragrance of the perfume. We gathered some fallen petals and took them to the little boating lake, where we scattered them into the water and watched them sail away as we made a wish. I wished I would be allowed to stay at the manse forever. Sadly, my wish was short-lived.

On our return to the manse, Auntie Marjorie explained that she would be taking me back to Rothwell after tea. Although I was repeatedly told I could come again the next weekend and stay from Friday night until Sunday, I was unable to comprehend why I had to return to the orphanage. I could hardly eat my tea as the tears flowed and I wiped them on my napkin. I did not want to leave this lovely peaceful home. I did not want to take off my new dress and put on my orphan's dress, so Auntie Marjorie allowed me to keep it on. My other clothes were packed, ready for my return. Uncle William said that as he would be conducting the evening service at the church he would not be able to travel with us. He kissed me and told me to be a good girl so that I could come to see them again next week.

I was so afraid. I had seen so many children beaten by Miss Silverwood after suffering rejection by foster aunts and uncles. I expected the same would happen to me. Surprisingly, Miss Green wanted to know if I had enjoyed my visit to the manse.

After Auntie Marjorie had said goodbye, I was hastily ushered into the locker room; against all my protests, my new dress was stripped off me and put in the staff cupboard. The usual night-time prayers were said as I knelt on the hard flagstones around the old black fire range. My hair was scraped through with the nitty comb. Sadly, I climbed the two flights of stairs to my iron bedstead and hard blankets. There was no silky blue eiderdown. I cried myself to sleep.

The next day, I was quiet. Inwardly, I tried to reason with my return. I could not think of anything I had done wrong. I waited the dreaded call to Miss Silverwood's office, but it never came. I had spent two wonderfully happy days in the big world outside the orphanage. I had seen such lovely things and, it is true, I had been the centre of attention with everyone I had met. Now I was once again just one in a large crowd. I could not stop crying as I tried to wash and dress. Ellen cuddled me and helped me with my chores before we both got ready for school.

At school, I was unable to concentrate on my lessons. The teacher called me to her desk and she listened to the account of my first weekend at the manse. Together, we made a calendar so I could tick off the days to Friday. It was a long week for me, with very high levels of anxiety. I feared I would be another permanently returned child.

★★★

Five ticks later on the calendar and the school week was over, and I was dressed in my new underwear and lovely blue dress once more. Looking through the hall window, I was so excited when I saw Uncle William approaching the home.

Within a few minutes, I was on my way again to the manse and received such a warm welcome. Upstairs in my bedroom, lying on the blue silk eiderdown, was a little doll dressed in pink knitted clothes and wrapped in a white lacy shawl. As I lifted it up, Auntie Marjorie said, 'Darling, you can keep the dolly. What would you like to call it?'

I do not know why I called my doll Margaret; I just liked the name. I immediately tucked my doll into the bed next to the one I had chosen to sleep in on my first visit. Thereafter, when bedtime prayers were said at the manse, I knelt down by my doll's bed so she could hear my prayers. I always ended my prayer by saying, 'Please, Jesus, help me find baby Kevin.' Uncle William asked me to share with him and Auntie Marjorie my memories of Kevin. I told them about his red hair, big blue eyes and dirty shawl. He listened and smiled.

On Saturday morning, we returned to Leeds and visited Schofields shoe department. I was asked to put my feet into a special machine and told to look through the glass at the top. Auntie Marjorie explained that this would tell the assistant what size shoes I required. Mesmerised by the X-ray effect, I wanted to know what other bones were inside my body. This experience opened up new horizons for me (perhaps this was the start of my interest in human biology). I chose a pair of black patent shoes with straps across the front and was delighted when my heavy orphanage shoes were put into the bag and the new stylish ones were left on my feet.

I spent the first part of the afternoon in Uncle's study. We played snap and dominoes, before I was distracted by the sound of very heavy rain beating against the bay window. I rushed over to the window to watch the rainstorm. Suddenly, there was a little face peering in at me. I put my tongue out at it, and then ran to tell Auntie and Uncle, who came to investigate. The front door opened, and in came a very wet and bedraggled person whom I recognised as Agnes, the little lady who had sat next to me in the church the previous week. Under her arm she carried a brown paper parcel neatly tied up with string. I asked her what she had brought me.

'Something very special', said Agnes.

Eagerly, I waited until Agnes had hung her wet coat to dry on a wooden clothes horse near the fire. The string on the parcel was carefully removed and set aside, and the brown paper neatly folded. I was very disappointed to see there was only a long piece of grey material inside. Disgruntled, I went upstairs and played with my doll. After a little while, I was called back into the room. I was asked to stand still while a tape measure was wound around many parts of my body. Agnes drew a picture of a little girl on a piece of paper and wrote down some numbers. At last, the tape measure was stored away, and tea served. The next day Agnes was sitting in the church when we arrived. I took hold of her hand and asked her if I could call her 'Auntie Agnes'. She smiled, cuddled me and said, 'I will be very proud to be called Auntie.'

★★★

Sunday evening soon came around again, bringing with it more tears, more dress changes and the new shoes locked in the staff room cupboard. Another week at school brought the same reaction: tears, uncertainty and the daily ticks on the calendar until Friday evening came around again.

As Chaplain of St George's Hospital, Uncle was able to time his visits to coincide on Friday with the end of the school day. He always arrived at the orphanage just before teatime. As we travelled on the tram, Uncle William told me he had received a letter from the Social Work Headquarters, confirming permission had been granted allowing me to have regular weekend visits to the manse.

Auntie Marjorie always had delicious, freshly baked scones with homemade jam ready on the table. One weekend, Auntie Agnes arrived after tea. This time, she allowed me to open the brown paper parcel. The length of grey material had been transformed into a beautiful, grey double-breasted coat. I put it on and threw myself into her arms to say, 'thank you'. Slipping my hands into the pocket there was a lacy

This is the earliest photograph I have of myself, aged five. I am wearing the little grey coat that Auntie Agnes made for me.

handkerchief with my name embroidered on one corner. There was also a silver sixpence.

I was told the coat was a present from Auntie and Uncle. The gifts in the pocket were from Auntie Agnes. The fact that Auntie Agnes had actually made the coat for me sealed a bond of love between us and, from that day, Agnes became someone very special to me.

The weekends were times of real happiness, until Sunday night when the tears would flow and I would be returned to Rothwell. On Monday mornings, my black gymslip replaced my finery until the next weekend. This routine continued for many months. I adored my new auntie and uncle, but could not understand why other children, who had been taken out in a similar manner were usually permanently fostered, adopted or, sadly, sometimes totally rejected.

I repeatedly questioned why I was always taken back to Rothwell before the Sunday evening service began at the church. I knew I had not done anything wrong at the manse. When Auntie Marjorie took me back, she always informed Miss Green or her assistants how good I had been. So, why did I have to live as an unwanted orphan from Monday until Friday, then after school be transported to a place of love, warmth and luxury?

I felt as though I lived in a topsy-turvy world. The day of the week was so important. It governed how I was going to be dressed, what I would eat, where I would sleep and, above all, if I would be loved, or not. The weekends were certainly times when great love and attention were lavished upon me. Monday to Friday became days of great uncertainty. Would I ever be loved again? Would Uncle come for me? Would I go to the manse again, or to the park? I hoped I would meet all those lovely people at the church who had showered me with the gifts of books and toys and almost constant attention.

The church congregation began to send parcels of toys, books and items of clothing for the other children who lived with me in Rothwell. Sometimes there would be sweets, which were always considered quite a luxury. Although these parcels were making me very popular with the girls in my dormitory, they often provoked jealousy from girls in other rooms. I easily became the target for their aggression. I learnt very quickly that I was only popular with the older children if I had something to give to them; otherwise, I was just another little child in the way.

Seven

LEEDS MARKET
AND SPECIAL OUTINGS

During several visits to the manse, Auntie Agnes cared for me if there were matters at the church needing the attention of the minister and his wife. Sometimes I was taken to Leeds market and I found this a fascinating place. Over its entrance was an ornate archway; beneath this, there was my favourite little kiosk, which sold the most delicious ice cream cones. I could only just reach the top of the counter. Very quickly, I learnt how to smile nicely at the owner, who would add an extra dollop of ice cream into the cone.

I loved all the green-painted decorative wrought-iron railings and the brass light fittings above the stalls. Large mirrors hung above the fruit stalls, reflecting the wide range of fruit and vegetables displayed below. There seemed to be so many people milling around. They were friendly, happy folk who did not appear to be in a hurry.

The market stallholders would shout out their wares: 'Great juicy oranges luv! I've got a few bananas as long as yer legs, cabbages as big as yer 'eads! Come on luv, buy um today and I'll throw in some spuds.' I loved to watch as the purchased goods were placed into brown bags. With a quick flick of the wrist, the corners of the bag would be twisted and closed with such dexterity, and the next customer served.

Many of the flower stalls were just inside the huge front doors. The wonderful colours and the vast variety of flowers available fascinated me. There were also floral wreaths prepared, I was told, for funerals. Again, I thought of my mother and wondered if anyone had bought her a wreath. I secretly reasoned that, perhaps, when I found her grave, I could buy a wreath especially for her.

The fragrance of all the colourful blooms contrasted so sharply with the smells of the meat and fish stalls. There was the tripe stall, with its array of honeycombed white tripe with jelly that glistened under the lights – and where the plump owner always winked at Auntie Agnes and she coyly smiled back at him. The stalls lined the two long aisles, which led you though to the back of the covered market and out to the open-air market at the rear.

Here, you could buy almost anything. There were stalls selling pots and pans, electrical goods, carpets, nuts and bolts, packets of biscuits, or brown bags of broken biscuits at half the price. There were cheese stalls with their little tasty samples of cheeses from the Yorkshire Dales or more distant places.

Another stall sold remnants of very pretty materials, cotton reels, buttons and zips. Occasionally, Auntie Agnes would let me chose a length of material suitable for her to make into a dress for me to wear on my visits to the manse. Sometimes, I found it very difficult to choose from such a wide variety of colours and patterns. On one occasion, while I was looking through the bundles of material, I came across a length of cotton cloth with little pink elephants in white circles like clouds floating in the sky. I thought it was lovely. I was so disappointed when the piece left on the roll was not enough for a dress, so I chose a colourful floral pattern.

The next time I visited the market, I was wearing the dress Auntie Agnes made for me. The woman on the stall admired it and then handed Agnes a parcel. I was not allowed to know what was inside and, as time went by, I stopped asking questions and forgot about it.

Auntie Marjorie enjoyed knitting and often made me cardigans to match the dresses made by Agnes. Some of the women in the church congregation knitted or sewed garments for us to take back to the homes for the other girls. These clothes were always reserved for Sunday best. Miss Green always insisted that the girls sent letters of thanks.

I soon discovered that I was the envy of the other children. I am sure some children secretly envied the attention that was lavished upon me, especially by Miss Green, as she dressed me ready to go out on Friday night. Others showed frustration and anger at what they saw as favouritism. One or two older children vented this anger at me on Sunday evenings when I was no longer clad in my finery. I was often subjected to their punches, pushes and, on one occasion, I can vividly recall my new dress was torn before it reached the staff cupboard.

When Uncle William collected me the following week, he was informed my dress had been caught on some wire. I was afraid to say what had really happened, fearing I might not be taken out again. If Miss Silverwood, the matron of the home, had seen the tear, the perpetrator of the torn dress and I would certainly have incurred her anger and subsequent punishment.

I did not know what reaction I would encounter from my foster aunt and uncle. Agnes was called to the manse to repair my dress. I was asked if I had hurt myself on the wire, and she said she would kiss it better. Suddenly, I felt awful knowing I had told a lie. Sensing my guilt, Auntie Agnes assured me it was not wrong to tell the truth; she would not punish me if the dress had been torn accidentally or by others. I told the truth and a piece of embroidery appliqué was placed over the tear and a valuable lesson learnt. 'Tell the truth and shun the devil,' said Auntie Agnes. I had no idea who this devil was, but 'Ooh, yer little devil' was a favourite description of any misbehaving child in Rothwell.

★★★

My visits to the Legassicks and the contact with the church proved beneficial to the orphanage. Several social groups began fundraising for special outings. The Girl Guides collected toys for distribution to the children in our home. Some of the men made large wooden sit-on lorries and scooters for the boys' home. When these items were delivered, I was the star attraction, and no punches came my way. Local people and the church groups got together and arranged an outing for all the children from all four houses.

We were up early on Bank Holiday Monday and completed our tasks, before dressing in our very best outfits. My dress was made of beautiful blue silk material, another one of Auntie Agnes's creations. The day was warm and sunny, so thankfully no coats and berets were required.

Suddenly, there were squeals of delight as a long row of taxis drew up outside the huge black gates. From the taxi doors and windows colourful streamers gaily flew in the gentle breeze. Balloons bobbed up and down at the back of each vehicle. The drivers wore fancy hats and provided each child with one to match theirs. Each vehicle had its own colour scheme. We were told to remember the colour, so we could return to the taxi if we happened to get lost in the crowd.

Miss Green made sure her charges stayed together! Her discipline paid dividends. We were ordered to line up in Sunday crocodile fashion and await her instructions before the journey began. When all the children were seated, the taxis began the journey out of Rothwell towards the centre of Leeds. The long procession wound its way up Briggate, one of the main streets in Leeds city centre, and out towards Roundhay Park. We felt so happy and very excited at being the centre of attention for the day. Suddenly, it seemed as if being an orphan brought some rewards other children in Rothwell village did not get. Passers-by stopped to wave and cheer us on our way. We felt very special as we waved back.

At the park, the Lord Mayor of Leeds and all the volunteers who had made the event possible greeted us. One section of the park is known as the Roman Hill. Here, a steep step formation rises up to form a large grassy seating area, ideal for such a crowd of children.

Each child received a bag containing an individual pork pie, a sausage roll, sandwiches and, best of all, a bun with icing on top. However, there was no escaping grace before we were allowed to eat as the vicar of Holy Trinity Church Rothwell had travelled with our retinue. He blessed the food with such a booming voice that even those sitting at the top of the Roman Hill could hear it.

Organised games took take place in the auditorium. Those not taking part could watch without leaving their seats. Competitions between the different houses proved very popular and bags of sweets were handed to the winning team, to be later shared out among the fortunate house occupants. I remember having to take part in the sack race. There was no way I would be a winner as I was the smallest child, but as so many older children fell over, it did mean I came in just before the last competitor and was quite proud of this fact. This had, after all, been my first race in life, and I had enjoyed it so much. Indeed, the whole day had given so many children such happiness.

We returned home exhausted, but despite our tiredness, there was no escaping the nitty comb and ritual prayer time before bed. The next day on the rota board, a list of the prize-winners was displayed for all to see. Miss Green shared out the sweets in our home, but we heard from the occupants of the other homes that they never got their sweet reward. It seemed the staff had withheld them.

★★★

Ellen told me I had to share my sweets with a little girl who had just come into care and now walked to school with me. Looking back, I am so glad I did as I was told, because a few weeks after our trip to Roundhay Park, we were all confined to our dormitories.

We were unable to attend school and from our window we watched as an ambulance came and parked outside the front doors. We saw a little body wrapped in a red blanket carried out in the arms of the ambulance man and gently laid in the back of the vehicle. It was my little school friend.

For the first few days of her illness, she had been kept in the isolation room. We heard rumours that she had scarlet fever. In silence, we watched as the ambulance drove off at speed, taking her to Seacroft Isolation Hospital. A few days later, we heard of the death of this little child. I remember standing by the window alone one day, wondering if the little girl's mother had at last come to take her home. I stood there in my loneliness and cried. A doctor examined all the children and the strict segregation of one household was enforced.

When no one showed any sign of illness, we were eventually allowed out of quarantine. Surprisingly, we were very glad to return to our classes. School was a place where no hard tasks had to be completed and most of the teachers were very kind to us. Even the local children respected our strength-in-numbers strategy, although we were still known as the 'orphans from the bad kids' home'. The trauma of recent days did bring about a general sadness over the village of Rothwell. At the school assembly, the headmistress prayed for the child and all the children in Rothwell Children's Home. These prayers made us aware that others in the community were saddened by the child's death. We were not entirely unknown, just unwanted.

The fear and terror that this little one's death brought to the rest of the orphans was immense. At night after lights out, we lay awake talking about what death was. No one seemed to know the answer. Some of the older children who had come into care during or after the war could give details of seeing dead family members, or dead people from their communities. Often, highly graphic accounts were related as we lay there in the darkened room. I recall asking if my mother had died in the war. Older girls reassured me I was born after the war and therefore, my mother must have been alive in 1946 and not bombed to death. Here was my first clue to my grave hunts. I would have to remember when I was born and look for a grave dated thereafter.

★★★

It was so sad to hear the stories some of the teenage girls could tell of the war years. One girl had been left crippled when a bomb had fallen near her parents' home. Her mother had been killed and her father had disappeared fighting overseas. We heard how happy she had been when she lived with her mother and father and what good parents they had been.

Two older girls had been evacuees, their homes destroyed in the war and their parents were missing. Both girls spoke of happier days with their own loved ones. It seemed the war had left many orphans, which might explain why there were such large numbers of children in care.

Many of our deeper fears and worries were discussed in the dormitory at night. Together, we would all sing to the tune 'When Irish Eyes Are Smiling' the following words:

It was in a foreign prison,
Where a British soldier lay,
And wrote home to his mother,
Who was very far away:
'Dear Mother, when I go to heaven,
Will the angels let me stay?
Or just because I am now a cripple,
Will they say I am in the way?'

How the tears would flow after we had sung this song and we would cry ourselves to sleep.

There were occasions when the singing would be more light hearted. 'Old McDonald had a Farm' brought hoots of laughter as we each made the animal noises. I always liked doing the pig impersonation. My 'oink, oinks' echoed around the room, and my meows would make any Cheshire smile. The cacophony of moos perhaps should have been replaced with boos, but the other occupants of my dormitory did not seem to mind my tuneless vocal attempts, nor did the staff object to the night-time singing. They were probably enjoying their supper in peace in the staffroom, away from hordes of children.

***

No drinks were served after six o'clock each evening and we were never allowed to leave the dormitories. At bedtime after lights out the dormitory doors were locked for the night. Often, especially if we had sung or cried too long, we would be thirsty. The older girls showed the young ones how to suck the cold black-painted iron bed frame for a few minutes to encourage saliva to form in the mouth. I now wonder how many chemicals were also absorbed!

When it rained heavily outside, we would open the window, catch a few raindrops on our hands and suck these to quench our thirst. At the manse, I only had to ask nicely, and a glass of water was left on the bedside cabinet, in case I was thirsty before going to sleep. When I told this to the other children, they thought I was telling lies.

I was frequently subjected to more questions and sometimes this bordered on ridicule. One of the girls admired one of my lovely new dresses and I proudly announced my Auntie Agnes had made it. This answer brought an unexpected retort. I was asked, 'If your Auntie loved you so much as to make you a dress, why did she not take you home for good?'

Silence … I did not know the answers to these questions, and this caused me so much inward uncertainty and anxiety. Within me, there was terrible conflict. I could not reason at all with the stark contrasts of life. I questioned how someone could say that they loved me and constantly try to reassure me that I was wanted so much, and then return me to a place where there was no mother or father, aunt or uncle to comfort me. I could not understand why all the children, whom I liked so much and played with in the Sunday school, were allowed to stay in their homes all week, but I had to return to Rothwell from Sunday night until Friday.

Great conflicts were fought within my young mind as I tried to make sense of all the changes I had to cope with. The increasing number of stories I was hearing about the way that Jesus loved children also raised questions within: Why was love bestowed in abundance upon me at the weekend, then withdrawn on Sunday night? Was Jesus only for Sundays? When you went to church, did He know you were there? If so, was I only to be loved if I too went to church? How could I go to church on school days?

These inner questions went around my head, and I could find no answers. I was too young to try to decipher all the inner turmoil, but I was very aware of their presence and longed for someone with wisdom to help me. Neither did there seem to be anyone who could help me to find my baby brother, Kevin, who now seemed lost forever.

Eight

ROYALS AND MARKET TRADERS

The people of Rothwell and Leeds were always generous in their giving and we were the grateful recipients of their kindness. Various outings to cinemas and theatres were arranged for us and one of these special events was a visit to the City Varieties in the Headrow, Leeds.

This lovely old Victorian musical hall was able to accommodate all 150 children and staff. We had to dress in old-fashioned costumes, which added an extra dimension to all the excitement as we prepared for the evening show. Some of the costumes came from the theatre, others from the large costume box we had in the recreation hut. Outfits for the boys were created in the sewing room at the orphanage from materials donated by the Leeds market traders and from the numerous textile and tailoring companies in the city. Auntie Agnes and a few of the women from the church made some of the fancy-dress outfits for the girls in my dormitory. Some of the staff brought in fancy hats for us, which were tied on our heads with long braids of ribbon. We loved our colourful outfits and frolicked around the hall as we waited for the coaches to arrive to take us to Leeds.

Above the entrance to the old music hall flashing striped neon lights appeared to open and close like curtains, illuminating the narrow alleyway. Pictures of famous stars who had performed in the past and up-to-date pictures of the stars we were about to see were posted on the walls. A member of the staff had brought along her own child, who sat beside one of the boys. On seeing this stranger, the lad shouted at the top of his voice, 'Oi! this kids not one of us. Ees got a ma!' He got a sore lug for his trouble!

When the lights dimmed, a man dressed in a dark suit introduced the individual acts. He pulled off his white gloves so slowly and slapped them down with such force that we jumped in our seats. He used long words and funny sayings that raised a laugh with most of the audience, but the younger children, including myself, could not understand what he was telling us. We were very glad when he sat down and shut up!

Encouraged to sing along with the acts, we let our inhibitions go and thoroughly enjoyed ourselves. Halfway through the show, the lights went on and we lined up in crocodile form to use the toilets. Each child was given an ice cream before somehow returning to our exact seats in an orderly fashion. I personally loved the Tiller Girls' sparkling costumes and feathered plumes on their headdresses. I secretly dreamed of joining their troupe when I grew up. We were enthralled by everything we had seen. At the end of the show, we had to stand and sing 'God save our Gracious King'.

***

It would be the last time we would sing those words, as the next event I recall was that the king had died. The year 1952 was indeed a sad one for the country. In church on Sunday, the vicar informed us of the Royal Proclamation of our new young Queen Elizabeth, and prayers were said for the late king. Our next outing was a visit to the picture house in Rothwell to watch the king's funeral on the Pathé Gazette news.

Within a few weeks, we returned to the picture house and saw our first pictures of the uncrowned queen and Prince Philip playing with their children, Charles and Anne. For some of the children in care, these were the first pictures they had seen of parents with their families, and perhaps gave a much-idealised view of life beyond the orphanage gates. Despite this, we avidly collected all the news of the royal family. Staff brought in their old magazines, and some of the girls gathered pictures to put into scrapbooks that they had received as Christmas presents.

We swapped doubled-up pictures for others we had not yet found ourselves and I was able to bring back pictures gathered at the manse. Some of these I swapped and soon had a full book of such lovely family pictures. Not only were the scrapbooks popular, so were the discussions and hopes for handsome princes who would come and take us away from Rothwell.

The nearest we got to realising our dreams was a new photograph of Prince Philip in naval uniform. He was a real handsome prince, who made many a young heart flutter. Permission was granted for us to put up his picture on our dormitory wall. A lovely framed picture of the queen with the royal children was presented to us by the Rothwell Miners Club and hung in the dining room. We also received a portrait of Sir Winston Churchill, the prime minister. He looked so sternly down at us as we scrubbed the entrance hall. Miss Green was a real royalist and taught us to respect the role of the British royal family. She reminded us that if we ever married a prince, she wanted an invite to the wedding!

There was an air of great anticipation in the country, and we in the orphanage were equally swept along with the hope of better things to come. The radio programmes became lighter in content and tone. Miss Green sang happier tunes. We still had plenty of chores around the homes, but heavy bedding and sheets were now sent to the laundry in the village, thanks entirely to the old boiler system having given up the ghost and there being no available funds for its repair.

This may have lightened our physical load, but it also led to freezing cold bedrooms. Although we were allowed one extra blanket each, we still shivered at night. We waited until lights out and the door was locked before putting our socks back on and doubling our blankets in two to add extra warmth.

★★★

I lost my first tooth. I had heard if I put my baby tooth under my pillow, the tooth fairy would come and take it away and leave me a penny, so carefully I placed my little tooth under my pillow. On waking, I expectantly dived under the pillow to retrieve my penny. I cried when I realised the tooth fairy had not come to the orphanage. I never believed in fairies again.

Within the next few months, more teeth fell out. My new teeth were very slowly and painfully emerging, but there was no analgesic offered. Quite a few of the recently arrived younger children were also losing their first teeth. Mealtimes were rather comical as we gummed our way through thick crusts of bread or Sunday toast!

About this time, arrangements were made for me and several other children to attend the dental hospital in Fenton Street in the centre of Leeds on a regular basis. Dental students were assigned a child as part of their training course. As an adult, I now realise that these visits had a more profound personal benefit. Children in care often have little close human contact. The trainee dentist would perhaps, unknowingly, be satisfying a personal need within each child to receive a high level of care and individual attention.

★★★

There were many coal mines in and around the Rothwell area; the pithead wheels were visible for miles around, along with the huge concrete cooling towers. On our way to school or church, we would see miners trudging home after a hard day's work or nightshift, their faces still bearing traces of coal dust. Sadly, we became aware from conversations at school that some local men resented the fact that many of the miners had not served in the armed forces during the war. Their jobs in the mines had been considered essential wartime employment. These men were known as the Bevin Boys.

The men who had been in the forces were easily distinguishable by the demob suits, collars and ties. The Bevin Boys had no fancy suits as a reward for their hard work below ground. We heard of some bitter family feuds, especially where sons or brothers had been separated by their trades. These rivalries did not stop them from coming together and frequenting the miner's clubs, before returning home somewhat inebriated, especially after brown pay packets had been issued, but neither did the feuds prevent the community coming together for fundraising campaigns on our behalf.

The fundraising proceeds were used to take large groups of children to the seaside resorts around the Yorkshire coast. As these outings were always on Saturdays, they coincided with my days at the manse. I may have missed the coach rides, but I loved listening to my roommates' happy accounts of trips to the beach, fish and chips eaten out of newspapers, and bags of goodies to bring home. It was good to know others were able to escape the drudgery of Rothwell and enjoy happier times.

We certainly had many people to thank for their tremendous fundraising efforts, and time dedicated to making life in the orphanage more bearable. If only these same benefactors could have seen the sparse conditions in which we lived in inside the homes, I am sure they would have helped us, but our harsh treatment in Rothwell was hidden from view.

Nine

ELLEN, MUMPS
AND BIRTHDAY CAKE

Returning home from school one day, I was greeted in the hall by Ellen. She was smartly dressed in her Sunday best clothes. Her black beret, perched jauntily over her curly hair, framed her lovely face but failed to hide the falling tear trickling down her cheek. I cried bitterly when she told me she was leaving Rothwell for good.

A few weeks earlier I had watched her disappear through the front door with two people who had visited her on several occasions. Now I realised these same people must have been prospective foster parents. We both sensed this was to be our last farewell.

I felt so bereft of our friendship. Ellen had always been my support and guided me through the maze of rules and regulations. She had taught me how to survive in this confusing environment. I stood by the window and waved until the taxi was out of sight. In my heart, I wished Ellen all the happiness in the world, but I did not want her to leave me. Now, on weekdays, I would stand alone.

★★★

Nobody's Child

Within a very short time of this sad episode I found myself in the isolation room, having contracted mumps. I had no recollection of being transferred from the upstairs dormitory. I do remember having a blinding headache and not being able to swallow without pain in my throat. Visiting restrictions were in place and only members of staff were allowed into the room – even they did not come very often.

At first, I felt so ill that the days and nights seemed to merge, but gradually, as I began to recover, I was able to observe my surroundings. The isolation room was very large with dark brown wood panels on all four walls. Across the windows brown wooden shutters had been closed over, allowing only a small chink of light into the room. At night, the moon cast a thin silver streak on the opposite wall. Plates of food and drinks were left on the table near the door. If I was hungry or thirsty, I had to get up and take what I wanted.

On bed-changing day, I had to strip my bed and leave the bedding by the door. One of the assistants came and took it away and left clean sheets, which reeked of strong Lysol disinfectant. I barely had enough energy to put the clean sheets on the bed. There was only one bed in the room, but ample space to accommodate more beds if the need arose to isolate more sick children. A small, bare light bulb high on the ceiling cast an eerie glow around the room. The old black fire range had seen better days; it was not highly polished like the rest of the fireplaces in the main buildings. In the grate, newspapers and sticks that lay ready to light now looked damp and were thickly covered in fallen soot from the huge chimney breast. I asked if I could see Miss Green and was told she was on sick leave.

One night, I had an awful dream. I dreamt that Uncle William was kneeling down by the only chair in the room. He was wearing his clerical dog collar and was pointing a finger in the air. Auntie Marjorie was standing by my bed knitting while Auntie Agnes was holding a towel in both hands as if waiting to catch me if I fell out of bed. All their faces seemed huge. This dream left me terrified. It had been so vivid that I asked many times during my childhood if it had been real.

Auntie Agnes assured me that this must have been a bad dream, possibly the results of the crisis of the illness.

I spent my sixth birthday alone in this room. Aunt and Uncle had visited, but they were not allowed into the room to see me. They had brought a birthday cake for me. The assistant, whose responsibility it was to care for me, told me to stay on my bed. She brought the cake for me to see. Standing at the door, well away from me, she opened the white cardboard box and tilted it so I could see the contents. Inside, there was the most beautiful birthday cake. The white icing was edged with pink swirls and in the centre there were some pink roses made of icing. My real name, Gloria, had been piped on top beside a silver number six. I was so enthralled to see such a lovely cake. This was the first time I had had a birthday cake, and I was longing to have a piece and one of the pink roses to eat. It never came!

That was the last time I saw the birthday gift. After fully recovering and returning to the rest of the household, the other children told me that the cake went on to the staff table. It was not even shared out amongst some of my dormitory friends. Now, new emotions began to rise within me. I felt a sense of hatred for the assistant who had deprived me of a piece of my birthday cake. I could never recall before having such feelings and was rather unsure of how to handle this new emotion of anger.

The next time I was at the manse, I was brave enough to tell my aunt and uncle what had happened to their birthday gift and how I felt. They assured me it was a normal reaction to feel angry, but it was explained to me that anger must not be allowed to turn to hate. I was to forgive the assistant. But how could I forgive? She had not said she was sorry, and she had deprived me of my cake! I continued secretly to hate her.

The following weekend, Uncle William spoke to me about my feelings regarding the incident as we walked together to the park. He reiterated that I was to forgive the care assistant who had wronged me. This was easier said than done.

On our return from the park, there seemed to be an air of excitement in the house. I soon discovered, in my absence, children from my

Sunday school class had gathered. The dining room table was spread with lots of lovely things to eat. In the centre, there was another birthday cake. It was not as pretty as the one I had been deprived of, but it did have little sweets on top and a silver number six. I was given a big piece of cake and several jelly sweets. I learnt that the two aunties had got together and made it for me.

After tea, we all played games and at the end of the party, each visiting child received some sweets and a piece of cake to take home. When the guests had left, Auntie Agnes produced another brown paper parcel for me to open. Inside was a wonderful surprise.

Somehow, she had purchased enough material with the pink elephants on the white clouds, which I had so admired on the market stall. I was now the very proud owner of a lovely dress with a little white Peter Pan collar and a pair of pants to match. I suddenly remembered the lady on the market stall giving Auntie Agnes a parcel – she had managed to get some more of the material. I put my new dress on, danced gaily around the room and lifted up the hem to show everyone my matching knickers. I refused to take the dress back to Rothwell; I did not want this lovely dress damaged.

A few weeks later, I arrived at the manse to find my doll lying in a beautiful navy-blue Silver Cross doll's pram. I was so excited when I discovered that Auntie Agnes had used some of the scraps of material left over from my pink dress to make dolls clothes and a beautiful patchwork quilt and pillow. Auntie Marjorie had knitted some lacy blankets in lovely pastel colours and decorated them with tiny ribbons.

I insisted I wanted to take my pram and doll to church. Amazingly, permission was granted. However, I was not amused when I had to leave the pram in the vestibule until after the service. Uncle William seemed to talk for such a long time, and the hymns were so long. Even Sunday school, which I usually enjoyed so much, failed to hold my attention. At last I was reunited with my pram and doll and I insisted on pushing it by myself up the very steep Beeston Hill back to the manse. When the time came for me to return once more to the orphanage, I left my pram and doll in the study, ready for my next visit.

Ten

'Cos God Says So'

An Unseen Guest sat at the manse table; we said grace to Him. He also was in the church because the deacons offered the collection plate to Him. I could not understand why anyone wanted to be invisible or refuse to take the money offered. After all, I thought it was wonderful when people gave me a threepenny bit or, even better still, a silver sixpence. I was not afraid to be seen, and my piggy bank grew to bursting within a very short time.

Uncle William advised me to save some of the monetary gifts I received and took me to the Yorkshire Penny Bank, where I was instructed to hand over my money along with a little bank book. I was very disgruntled when only the book was returned to me and promptly, in a loud voice, told the woman behind the counter, 'It's wrong to steal, cos God says so.' Uncle William was insistent that I apologised, but I stubbornly refused. The woman had taken my money!

Sometime later, when I returned to the bank, my bank book and a bag containing several ten-shilling notes and some coins were handed to me. Only then did I realise the woman had not really stolen my money. Again, Uncle explained to me that the woman had been saving it for me and, because I had put it in the bank, a little interest would be added to my account. This I liked very much.

Uncle had not forgotten my previous misdemeanour and entreated me to apologise for my mistrust of the bank person. Hugging my first money bag, I said I was sorry. I was not let off so lightly, though, for my errant ways. I had to put a few coins in the missionary box at the church, so my first interest was reduced. Arriving back at the manse, I was encouraged to put my treasure into Uncle's desk for safekeeping.

The next day I had a wonderful surprise. After church, I was so ecstatic when I was told I would not be going back to Rothwell that evening as usual. Permission had been granted for me to stay with Auntie and Uncle for a week and we were going on a holiday together.

I was so excited when Auntie Agnes came to the manse to look after me. I told her my good news. Together, we gathered my clothes and packed them into a brand-new suitcase. However, suddenly, when I saw the case placed by the front door, my insecurities mounted. I had seen so many packed cases at Rothwell's front door. Friends I had made in the dormitories had literally disappeared. Would I ever see any of them again? I definitely wanted to leave Rothwell Orphanage, but I felt afraid of the unknown and questioned why Auntie Agnes was not going with me.

I burst into tears. Auntie Agnes lifted me onto her knee and comfortingly assured me she knew exactly where I was going. I was going to meet Auntie Marjorie's sister, who was called Nester Ryland. Auntie Agnes explained how she was once the personal maid to Mr and Mrs Ryland, Auntie Marjorie's parents. They had lived in a large house on a hill in Leighton Buzzard, Bedfordshire. Auntie Agnes had eventually left their service and returned to Leeds to care for her ageing father.

★★★

Arriving at Leeds Station, I was amazed at the sight of the gigantic hissing monster that was to pull the train to our destination, but once on board, sitting comfortably on the plush red seat beside the window, my initial fears subsided as I listened to the sounds of clickety-clack, clickety-clack as the wheels rumbled along the track.

It turned out Old McDonald's cows were real – I saw them! It is hard to believe now that I had never seen a horse or a cow before this holiday nor seen so many green fields and beautiful trees. I had seen flowers in the markets, parks or church buildings, but never seen whole swathes of them growing along the railway lines. Suddenly, my world became large and very beautiful. I wanted to live in the country and leave behind Rothwell homes forever.

I had a wonderful holiday staying in Nester Ryland's beautiful bungalow, surrounded by a most colourful cottage-style garden. I was thoroughly spoilt by all the Ryland family and Nester shared so many interesting accounts of her family's history.

The Rylands had been the proud owners of a large department store in Lake Street, Leighton Buzzard, and Auntie Marjorie had trained as a Norland nursery nurse. She had given up the opportunity of a good career to work with the Missionary Service in China before ill health had forced her to return to her family. Uncle William had been at Regent's Park College, studying Greek. His lecturer had wanted him to stay and continue his studies due to the high marks he was attaining, but he chose the ministry. His first church had been in Cardiff, south Wales, before he moved to Hockcliffe Street Baptist Church in Leighton Buzzard, where he met and married Marjorie. Their next church was Beeston Hill, in Leeds and here they had renewed their friendship with Agnes.

On Sunday, we attended the service at the church. I was introduced to a lady called Doris Dean, who had been a good friend to Agnes during her stay with the Rylands. Doris was such a lovely person and I liked her instantly. Before leaving, Doris asked if I would take a parcel of hand-knitted jumpers back to the homes. I asked her if I could come again to see her. 'Anytime my dear,' she said, 'Anytime.'

I was very sad when I had to bid farewell to everyone and return to Leeds. Tired from the long train journey, I was glad to arrive back at the manse and soon fell asleep under my blue silk eiderdown. At

Sunday school the following day, I told the class all the lovely things I had seen and heard. I shared with them the extreme joy I had experienced.

In the evening, I said my usual goodbye to Uncle William as he left the manse to conduct the evening service and I travelled back to Rothwell with Auntie Marjorie. I recall Auntie Marjorie telling me that it would be some time before I would see her again. Five days until Friday always seemed a long time, so I would go to school and tick each day off my calendar.

***

The next day, as soon as the school bell rang I rushed in to the teacher and shared with her my holiday activities. As always, she listened to me. I then went to my calendar board to place my first tick of the week over Monday's date. To my utter dismay, my calendar had been taken down. When I asked where it was, I was informed it was no longer required. No further details were given, so I decided I would make ticks on my jotter cover until Friday. Five marks on my jotter indicated that Friday had come at last. I rushed home and along the corridor to the staff room.

I panicked when I saw the closed door. I knocked and waited, but no one opened the door. Realising I had only a short time to get ready before Uncle William would arrive, I dashed upstairs and washed before returning to the staff room. There was still no response. This was the first time I had been left waiting to change out of my school clothes and into my manse outfit. I knew Miss Green had been on duty at breakfast time, so I went to look for her. I searched everywhere and could not find her.

I returned to the staff room and was horrified to see Miss Silverwood, waiting at the door. Without saying anything, she grabbed me by the collar of my school blouse and dragged me along the corridor towards the laundry. I could hardly breathe as she tightened her grip on me. Then, without any warning, she began to punch me and slap me across my face with such force that I was unable to stand. I dragged myself across the floor and tried to escape from her.

I was no match for her strength and violence. I screamed and screamed, but no one came to my aid. 'I'll make you scream!' she shouted, as more punches came my way. 'You wicked evil bitch. No wonder they don't want you.'

'Who doesn't want me?' I shouted.

Raising her hand to me again, she slapped my face and said, 'The Legassicks.'

Surely there was some mistake. The Legassicks loved me. How often had I heard them tell me how special I was to them?

I heard Miss Silverwood say, 'You want the moon, and they don't want you. Go to your dormitory and stay there.'

I stumbled back along the corridor and up the stairs. I threw myself onto my bed. It was as though a dark cloud had descended upon me. I heard the sound of the gong, which signalled it was teatime. I knew, if Uncle William had come for me, we would have been away before the call to come in for tea sounded.

Painfully, I made my way to the fire escape door. I looked out to see if I could see him. There was no one in sight. All I could see was what looked like halos around the gas lamps and the blurred outline of the tall square tower and chimney beside the laundry buildings.

Darkness began to fall. I was still standing by the door when the other children came to bed. Several tried to comfort me, but the tears kept falling. I stayed by the fire door for what seemed like eternity until, at last, the cold and utter exhaustion drove me to my bed. No one had prepared me for this horrendous trauma.

Little did I know then that the holiday I had so enjoyed signalled the end of visits to the Legassicks. The weekend was to be the last time I would stay at Cranbrook Avenue. I cannot recall anyone telling me I would never again enjoy the comfort and warm loving environment of the manse, or sleep beneath my lovely blue silk eiderdown. The only thing I knew I had done wrong was my conversation with the woman in the bank. Had my words, 'Cos God said so' cost me so much?

I eventually fell asleep beneath my two hard, grey blankets. The next morning I was awake when the staff entered the dormitory and shouted to us to get up. I was horrified when I discovered that I had no Saturday clothes. The girl who distributed the clothes to us had not known that I would be there – after all, I was never normally there on Saturday. I had no other option than to put on my black school gymslip, even though I knew it was against regulations to wear school clothes on Saturdays.

I entered the dining room to catcalls and ribaldry. A member of staff came towards me and dragged me off to the laundry corridor again. I was made to fill a bucket with cold water and told to wash all the green tiles along the corridor with the strong-smelling pink bars of carbolic soap. It was such a long corridor. The upper tiles were cream and well above my reach. The lower dark green tiles were very shiny and arranged in a pattern like house bricks. The task was so monotonous.

My body was sore from the previous night's beating. I was so exhausted I could hardly keep awake. I spent the whole day on my knees trying to complete the task. As darkness began to fall, I was sent to bed. I had been offered nothing to eat or drink all day. The only break I had been allowed was a visit to the toilet, and even there I had been supervised and could not drink from the taps. A chalk mark had been drawn on the floor so I would know where I left off. There were to be no tiles left unwashed.

At least I had escaped another beating. On my way to the dormitory, I passed a large cupboard with mirrored doors. The reflection of a very sad and forlorn little six-year-old child looked back at me.

A nobody's child in a black gymslip.

Eleven

TOO CLOSE TO THE MANSE

I was transferred to the Isolation Room with swellings in my fingers and right shoulder. My forearms were red and inflamed with the caustic effects of the carbolic soap that I had used to wash the tiles along the corridor. Miss Green came to see me. She looked at my arms and I saw the tears in her eyes.

I was informed that Miss Silverwood was starting her days off and would not be back for a week. Now, at least, I knew I would receive some kindness. One of the girls brought me a hot drink and some biscuits before she left to change into her Sunday clothes. I could only eat and drink slowly as my mouth was so bruised with the beatings I had endured. The house became quiet as all the residents left for church. The cook came into the room and assured me she would look in later to see if I needed anything. Hearing these words of assurance made me cry. Cook took me in her arms and wiped the tears away. I settled down without fear for some much-needed sleep.

After the bruises had healed, I returned to school. Every day I continued to mark my jotter with five marks and waited every Friday evening in the hope I would see Uncle William coming through the gates. He never came again to Rothwell. I felt so very sad and alone. Loneliness in a crowded room is hard to comprehend, but I was one of many who had outward contact but inward emptiness.

★★★

Within a few weeks, I found myself on my way with Miss Goddard to Beeston Hill. I was excited as we alighted from the tram and made our way towards the manse – I was sure Auntie Marjorie and Uncle William would be there waiting for me. When we passed the end of Cranbrook Avenue, I tugged at Miss Goddard's coat sleeve to tell her she was going the wrong way. 'No, we are not!' she snapped as we proceeded to walk up Dawson Avenue, the street that backed onto Cranbrook Avenue.

We walked to the house where the Wilsons lived. 'You are going to live here in future,' said Miss Goddard, as she handed me over to Mrs Wilson. Papers were hastily signed and my care worker left without offering me any explanation.

Although I was delighted to see Mrs Wilson, and later in the day Mr Wilson and Alan, I was very bewildered as to what was happening. I rushed over to the window and pulled back the pretty lace curtains I had so often seen from the manse bedroom window. I looked out across the back street to where I could see the back door of the manse. I was horrified to see a huge pile of wood and bricks on Uncle's tidy little back yard and was informed that the manse was being prepared for the new minister. I asked if I could go and see Auntie and Uncle.

Mrs Wilson explained they no longer lived in Leeds; they had moved to a place called Cheltenham. Somehow, I held back the tears. No one had told me that the Legassicks had actually left the area and the church. The Wilsons were to care for me now. Mrs Wilson said I was to call her 'Mummy'. I absolutely refused. In fact, I refused to do anything she asked. I really did think she was telling me lies about the manse and all the preparations taking place over the road. I could not comprehend that Auntie Marjorie and Uncle William would go away and leave me without telling me what was going to happen.

At first, when I heard this news, I was so sad, but within me there was also real anger welling up. I loved them. Did they no longer love me?

That night I was put to bed in the same room as Alan. I protested very strongly – I was not allowed in boys' bedrooms. This was not just awkwardness on my part. It was a punishable offence in Rothwell, and I feared Miss Silverwood's wrath. However, there was nowhere else to sleep. The Wilsons' house was identical to the manse and only had two bedrooms.

The next day, I was enrolled in Crossflatts Primary School and introduced to new teachers. Alan was in my class and looked after me, but I was very unhappy. Within a few days, I was moved out of Alan's class and joined girls my own age.

Seeing the manse door ajar one day, I ran across the back street into the house, past the builders and upstairs to my bedroom. There was no furniture, no Margaret doll, and no blue silk eiderdown. There was nothing but a pile of wood in one corner. I was stunned. I faced the reality of the situation with bursts of temper and aggression towards anyone who tried to console me.

The Wilsons were unable to go to church because of my behaviour. They did try everything to ease this awful situation for me, but they could not change the circumstances. Miss Goddard revisited me and told me to behave. Such a lack of wisdom left me very emotionally scarred. I hated her for her actions for many years to come, until I was able to analyse the events through adult eyes.

★★★

The Senior Children's Officer visited the Wilsons and as a result he transferred me back to Rothwell. When he left, I received another severe beating at the hands of Miss Silverwood. I returned to Rothwell School to find I had moved up a class and had a new teacher. I never saw Miss Goddard again.

Around this time in my life, I became very consciously aware of a Great Presence beyond my understanding. I did not hear or see anything. I just felt a real sense of inner peace. The traumas and beatings left me so exhausted, but sleep did not come easily. I would curl up in the foetal position and imagine I was being cuddled in someone's arms. I called this presence 'My Unseen Guest', who became very real to me.

My manse, church and Sunday school experiences all indicated that there was 'Someone', bigger and far greater than I am, who did care for me. In the darkest hours, often when the pain was at its worst, I would hold on tight in my mind to this Guest, until sleep would come at last and give me quiet peace. The frequency of these moments increased with every violent encounter with Miss Silverwood, or at times when it seemed I was being rejected by society.

The amazing thing was I really did feel a sense of comfort from these moments. I began to share my thoughts and feelings with my Unseen Guest, whom I now call Jesus. Perhaps this was early praying without others prompting me. Certainly, Kevin was part of these moments, and I would earnestly ask that someday I would find my baby brother. I did not share these moments with any of the girls or staff for fear I would be ridiculed. Even though we all attended church together on Sundays, heard stories about Jesus, and during the week used His name in grace before eating, some of the other girls lacked faith in God's existence.

The days passed into weeks, and I just became part of institutional life again. I had no gifts to share with the other children, neither had they gifts to share with me. We had to accept each other on face value.

***

Saturday dawned like any other day. I was on bedroom floor scrubbing duties, when Miss Green came and told me I had to put on my Sunday dress after dinner. All morning I wondered where I was going this time. As soon as lunch was over, I carried out her instructions and returned to the front hall with feelings of uncertainty.

Miss Green joined me and obviously realised my fears; she assured me all would be well. Within moments of hearing her words, I looked out of the window. There was Auntie Agnes coming up the drive, pushing my Silver Cross doll's pram. Miss Green opened the door, and I rushed out into the arms of Auntie Agnes. I was so overwhelmed, I cried such tears of joy.

Permission was granted for me to go out for the afternoon. Auntie Agnes was wise enough to tell me she could only stay for a few hours, but what happy hours they were! Together, we pushed my pram and the new doll that lay inside it to Rothwell Park. Despite living in the area, I had never been to this beautiful park before. The rhododendrons were in full bloom, and Auntie Agnes took a photograph of me standing by them. Her little Box Brownie camera fascinated me. I tried to take a picture of her and was disappointed when I could not see the results straight away. I was taken to a little green wooden building called 'the Kiosk', where I was allowed to choose threepennies' worth of sweets. Before returning to the orphanage, I was assured by Auntie Agnes she would return the following Saturday and we would visit the park again.

The long week passed, but not without fear. 'Mr Nobody' had slashed my lovely pram hood. Miss Green was furious and punished everyone because the culprit would not own up. Even I got extra chores to do. I remembered my torn dress and how Auntie Agnes had taught me to tell the truth. As soon as I saw her coming through the gates again, I rushed out and shared with her what had happened to my pram. I saw the look of disappointment on her face; she had after all walked all the way from Leeds to Rothwell pushing my pram only a week earlier. Her only response was to say, 'Whoever did that was very naughty.' I felt so sorry for Auntie Agnes; she had only tried to bring me some comfort.

A few weeks later my pram was taken away to be repaired, but it never looked as lovely again. However, it was very well used by so many of the children as it became to them just another communal toy, even though I tried to hold on to it myself.

★★★

Saturday afternoons were now so special to me. Auntie Agnes kept every promise she made and always arrived on time for all visits. Gradually, the time spent with her was increased, and together we travelled further afield. I was thrilled when we revisited Leeds market. How the place evoked such memories of previous days. I was determined now to enjoy every moment of freedom away from Rothwell.

On our return journey, we would stop at the newspaper stand where Auntie bought her *Yorkshire Evening Post* from Stanley, the paper seller. Despite the fact that he always wore two coats, one on top of the other, he looked so cold. His dark hair he was plastered down with Brylcreem, giving it a greasy appearance. On rainy days, he pushed aside the raindrops that trickled down his unshaven face with fingers blackened with newspaper print. I watched as Auntie Agnes took from her purse some extra coins and placed them in Stanley's hand, telling him to go and get a warm cup of tea. I was to witness this act of kindness so many times and Stanley was not the only person who received a few coins; other paper sellers and homeless people received small gifts, but always with the same instruction to buy a warm cup of tea for themselves. I often wondered if the recipients of this dear lady's kindness would spend the money wisely.

One day, Auntie Agnes asked if I would like to go with her to Beeston Hill Cemetery as she wanted to put some flowers on her parents' grave. I had been there before on occasions, when she had been looking after me during my time at the manse. I had played around the gravestones, always looking for my mother's grave, while Auntie Agnes tidied the family grave or the graves of other people she had known who now had no relatives left to tend their plots.

Over the months, I had built up a real trust in Auntie Agnes, to such an extent that I was able to ask her to help me find my mother's grave. There was a moment of silence. I looked into this dear lady's face and saw tears welling up in her beautiful dark brown eyes. She reached her arms out and drew me closer to her, 'Child, what are you saying? Your mother is not dead.'

I briefly pulled away, and then threw myself back into the arms of this dear aunt. I instinctively knew I was hearing the truth, but the truth was hurting so badly. If she hadn't died, why had my mother left me? I related my first carer's words to Auntie Agnes. Together, we sat on her parents' grave and she explained how my mother had left my father and gone to live with another man. I heard how my father could not cope with two children and hold down a job.

My paternal grandmother had been approached to see if she could take us, but ill health had prevented this. Had Miss Goddard tried to reunite us? In that split second, my thoughts drifted back to the little old lady lying in the bed near the window, and her gift taken from beneath the tablecloth. Was this dear old lady my grandmother? I remembered her farewell kiss. Would I ever see her again?

Leaving Beeston Hill Cemetery, we crossed the road into Crossflatts Park, another familiar place. I asked if I could see the manse. Wisely, Auntie Agnes said, 'Another day.' My love for her deepened; she had told me the truth. I have always considered Auntie Agnes's honesty an act of real humanity and kindness. I no longer struggled with the circumstances of my admission into the care system. I was not an orphan just abandoned by my mother and too much for my father to cope with. In her great wisdom, Auntie Agnes assured me that neither Kevin nor I were to blame. There was no denial of Kevin's existence, but Auntie Agnes was unable to tell me where he was. She genuinely did not know his whereabouts.

I would now ask any reader of these memoirs to step many years ahead and read the letters I wrote but never sent to Miss Silverwood as a means of therapy. These letters will clearly relate the next chapter of my life in Rothwell and the outcome of such events. Forgive me if some facts are already known. The letters relate to the physical and mental trauma and the violent torture I suffered at the hands of Miss Silverwood, along with so many other children who were also abused by Miss Silverwood while supposedly in her care – if care is even the right word!

Twelve

AUNTIE AGNES

Everyone seemed to be frightened of the trip across the yard to Miss Silverwood's room. Certainly, any boy or girl returning from there would be crying, some even screaming, and all would then have to scrub floors or stairs amidst their tears. I hoped I would never have to go there. Alas, the day did come when I was forced to make the dreaded journey, and the only way I can share with the reader the events of that day is by writing this letter, after which I hope to recall some happier times:

Dear Miss Silverwood,

Years ago, you came into my life. I did not ask you to act as my carer, or as you probably wanted to be seen, as a surrogate mother figure to me. I had my own mother, albeit not very loyal, but she had given me life and my name. I would have preferred to be allowed the opportunity to stay within my own family circle, perhaps with some external oversight from the N.S.P.C.C. Together, my little brother Kevin and I could possibly have faced many problems of poverty. We may have suffered some verbal abuse, neglect and even physical abuse, but nothing to compare with the violence and abuse you meted out to me. My mother's abandonment and my father's neglect were totally unacceptable in the eyes of society, and warranted through the Courts, under the Children's Act, our removal into a safe, secure and protected environment.

Did you ever read the Act?

You may recall how under the Aunt and Uncle Scheme of the late forties and early fifties, foster families and homes were sought to offload the overload of children in care. Thankfully, I was part of that scheme and through it, into my life came Agnes Lowe, known affectionately as Auntie Agnes. The joy and happiness Agnes brought into my life, the security and comfort when I was in her company and the hope for better things to come, remains even today indescribable. Auntie Agnes was the only person who heard my cries for help and believed me when I shared with her the violent abuse you inflicted upon me. Sadly, it was also Auntie Agnes who, in my teenage years, had to cope with the mental scars left from the days when you sought your own gratification by beating me and other children in your care so mercilessly.

I was only four years old when we met for the first time, but in the next few years, I was to wish we had never met at all. Buffeted from pillar to post within the care system and so cruelly separated from my little brother Kevin, I had now arrived, bag and baggage, on your doorstep. How quickly I was to learn that Rothwell Children's Home was hell on earth, with only rare glimpses of light and hope for the bewildered child. I longed for a peaceful environment in which to live, grow and to be loved. By the time I was six years old, I wanted to die and leave the place of repression and the torture you inflicted upon me. The goodness and gentleness of Auntie Agnes kept me alive and gave me a glimmer of hope in such darkness. Small in stature and delicately built, Agnes could easily be lost in a crowd of taller people. Only the glistening shades of her auburn hair neatly rolled in the nape of her neck, her beautiful dark brown eyes, and her delightful cheery voice made people aware of her presence. The delight and joy I experienced as I ran to meet her as she came through the black wrought iron gates that surrounded the orphanage, and the feeling of absolute safety as she cuddled me in her arms contrasted so sharply from your violent aggression.

The few hours in her company were so happy and full of lovely surprises. One day, Auntie Agnes was aware of another child who looked sad and forlorn and obviously had no visitor, so she asked if Mary could join us on our visit to Rothwell

Park. Together we played happily amongst the flowerbeds and visited the Fiddler's Pond (named because it was shaped like a fiddle), where we fed the ducks with bread.

Whenever Auntie Agnes visited the home, she always carried a large wicker basket, neatly covered with a clean cloth, beneath which was stored the most delectable goodies. On this occasion, it was a white ceramic bowl filled to the brim with strawberries coated in sugar. We stopped at the kiosk, and pink and white ice cream was placed on top of the lovely red berries. Mary and I licked every available morsel from the little china dishes in which she served the fruit and the silver spoons were sucked clean before being carefully re-wrapped and replaced in the basket.

Free to romp and play, my newfound friend and I began to roll our bodies down the grassy slope, squealing and laughing as we desperately tried to be the first to reach level ground. Suddenly, without a known cause, my nose began to spurt blood. Alarmed at seeing, perhaps for the first time, blood pouring from me, and tasting the salty liquid in the back of my throat, I cried. My fears and alarm were soon quelled, as Auntie Agnes attended to my needs and brought the bleeding under control.

Soon, Mary and I were running through the park again, enjoying the delights of freedom and the open spaces. Only my stained dress indicated something had happened. That stained dress brought out the worst in you. After Auntie Agnes had said goodbye and promised to visit the following Saturday, you unleashed such violence upon me. Yelling and shouting at me, you accused me of causing an old lady such distress by my blooded nose and my blooded dress. Screaming at me that I was the most wicked, devil possessed child you had ever met, you punched me hard on my nose. I reeled backwards, and again you struck me with such ferocity that my nose began to gush with thick red blood. It ran down my face and dripped in such a flow onto the floor. Now in terrible pain and utter confusion, I tried to clean up the floor with my bare hands, but the bloody pool only increased in size. In rage, you pushed my face down into the sticky red mess. Suddenly my whole head ached as you continued to thump it on the floor. The blood covered my face, my hands and splattered in large rings onto my previously stained dress. I felt as though the whole room was spinning around as my painful little body hit the floor.

I called out to Auntie Agnes to save me, but Auntie was not there; she was travelling home on the tram. My little companion had hidden away in fear and trembling.

Miss Silverwood please read the Children's Act.

I pause to dry the tears on my adult face as I recall my first sight and taste of strawberries, ice cream and blood. Experiences of:

Evil and Goodness,
Violence and Gentleness,
Brutality and Kindness,
Despair and Hope,
Hate and Love,
Turmoil and Peace were eternally etched on my mind that day.

You violently abused me.
Agnes loved me.
You almost destroyed me mentally and physically.
Agnes prayed for God's healing of the terrible scars.

The contrasts are so stark. I can never erase the memories of your brutality.

What I, the adult, can do is to look beyond the brute to the real person called Miss Silverwood, who is now forgiven, but who …

… must read the Children's Act.

My second letter:

Dear Reader,

I pause as the floodgates open. Tears from the depths of a little girl's heart, but shed from adult eyes.

First, let me share with you, dear reader, the joy of Auntie Agnes's visit. Mary was so delighted Auntie had bought her a nice new handbag, and she had made me a lovely brown furry rabbit, which was holding an orange felt carrot in its paws. I was so thrilled with it and happily cuddled it as we once more made our way to Rothwell Park.

As evening drew nigh, we made our way past the old mill in the village of Rothwell and stopped at the kiosk where Auntie Agnes bought Mary and me a small bag of Thorn's toffees. Each sweetie was wrapped in blue and white paper on which was a picture of a little girl holding a box of sweets above a dog's head. Auntie Agnes read the caption to us, 'It's too good for you, Spot', which made us laugh. I soon ate all my sweets, but Mary on arriving back at the home put the remainder of her sweets in her locker.

Time has erased the memories of what games we played on that lovely sunny day. I do recall how happy we were to be free and away from the orphanage and enjoying the goodies from the Auntie's wicker basket.

Having said our goodbyes to Auntie Agnes and assured by her that she would return the following Saturday, she left to make her way home. Miss Green, my housemother, bathed me, prayers were said, my hair combed with the obligatory fine-toothed comb, then she tucked me into bed where I soon fell asleep clutching my furry rabbit.

Suddenly, I was woken by Miss Silverwood, as she pulled me by my hair onto the floor. She shouted, 'You thief, stealing Mary's sweets!'

She dragged me still by the hair along the wooden corridor, and then as I began to protest my innocence, she started to kick and beat me mercilessly. By the time we reached the stairs, she had hold of my legs and began to drag me down the stone staircase. My head and body were thumping hard against the stone steps. Every part of me was hurting. On reaching the last step, Miss Silverwood dragged me up on my feet and somehow my head hit the marble pillar in the centre of the hall. I was then taken into the boys' dining room.

There I was stripped of my nightdress, and the beatings with fists and kicking feet continued. I was screaming and screaming as each blow fell on my naked body and the pain intensified. Some of the boys were in the room finishing their chores. Miss Silverwood turned to them and shouted, 'Bring the fire buckets of water.' The boys took the three red water buckets that usually hung on hooks next to the three red buckets of sand by the kitchen door.

One by one, Miss Silverwood emptied the three buckets of icy cold water over me. I stopped screaming and felt a sudden deep sense of fear come over me; it felt like a deep breath that went in and would not come out again. I had felt this terrible feeling of fear before, when my little baby brother Kevin and I were so cruelly separated. Now shivering with cold and every part of my body in pain, I was dragged back upstairs and taken into a strange room, not my usual dormitory. The bedding was stripped off the bed and put in the corridor; I was bodily thrown onto the bed. Miss Silverwood shouted to someone to bring a bucket. I am not sure who brought it, but it was left in the middle of the room. I was told to use that as a toilet. The door was slammed shut. I was left alone in the dark.

[To this day, I have very clear memories of that night. Again, I must pause as I write to let the tears flow.]

The inside of my head felt like jelly wobbling about. My ears were buzzing, my eyes were stinging and all of me ached. The shadows of the trees outside the window seemed to be dancing on the walls. I could see the moon in the sky. Auntie Agnes said a man lived on the moon and, if you looked, you could see his face, so I stared at the moon hoping the man would come down and help me.

Nobody came.

Suddenly, as I lay there so cold, I heard very loud screaming and the sounds of Miss Silverwood shouting, 'You thief, you wicked thief.' I thought she was coming back to get me, so I hid under the bed and listened to all the screams. It sounded like one of the boys, but I did not know which boy it was. Mercifully, I must have fallen asleep, exhausted.

I next recall Miss Green, my housemother, and Mary lifting me up onto the bed, and covering me with woollen blankets. Mary cuddled me and said she would look after me. She said one of the boys had admitted he took the sweets, and he got a real beating for it. He was then locked in the cellar for the night. Now it felt as if the inside of my head was swollen. My eyes were also swollen; one would not open properly and, when I touched it, the pain was awful. I asked Mary where my rabbit was. She told me Miss Silverwood had thrown it into the fire. I cried and cried for my furry rabbit. Childlike, I thought it must have felt the burning fire on its body. The tears seemed to stay behind the swollen eyes like puddles which slowly seeped out on to my pillow. I don't know how long I was left in that room; it seemed a long time, but then it seemed a long time since I had arrived under the care of Miss Silverwood.

The following Saturday Auntie Agnes came as promised.

When she saw the bruises on my body, she cried. Leaving Mary and me in the hall, she went to find Miss Silverwood. I was too young to know the outcome of that meeting, or who the people were that went in and out of the office, but that day my case was at the door. I was taken to Auntie Agnes's own home and tucked up in a lovely big comfortable bed.

I can clearly remember Auntie Agnes sitting by my bedside sewing and telling me lovely stories about her parents who had been so kind. She assured me there were good people in the world and she hoped I would meet some of them very soon. A few days later, I had a new rabbit. I named it Bunny.

Auntie Agnes, More Precious Than Gold

Dear Auntie Agnes,
Only four foot nine tall,
Came to the children's home,
When I was so small.
Seeing me there, so sad and alone,
She took me out for the weekend,
And I stayed in her home.
She bathed me and dressed me,
In a dress that was new,
And tied up my auburn hair
With ribbons of blue.
We sat by the fireside
And toasted some bread,
She showed me my bedroom
And big comfy bed.
She promised to love me
As we knelt down to pray,
And I learnt to thank Jesus,
At the end of the day,
For the wonderful kindness,
And love so freely bestowed,
From one who showed mercy
More precious than gold.

Me, aged six, with my new doll. What started out as a happy day with Auntie Agnes at Rothwell Park, turned into a most traumatic event.

Dear Auntie Agnes, and Auntie Cissie (Eleanor) your sister, whose prayers for healing have now been answered, and whose love and care far outweighed that of my own parental family. To you I owe a deep debt of gratitude. I can only repay that debt by recalling your words, 'Gloria forgive Miss Silverwood'.

Forgiveness has given me inner peace, but memories still linger …

Thirteen

ANOTHER HOME, ANOTHER BED

My removal from Rothwell after Miss Silverwood's abuse had taken place at the weekend and had been so swift that there was no time to have all the compulsory paperwork required in hand. However, I later learned that because I received such excellent care from Auntie Agnes and had such a deep love for her, the on-call Duty Social Worker had applied to the Child Welfare Officer for permission to have me transferred temporarily into her care overnight.

Auntie Agnes explained to me that I would have to return to Rothwell for a few weeks. Arrangements had been made for me to be transferred to the smaller cottage home situated within the grounds. I knew this building well. It was a much smaller house with bay windows at the front, facing Wood Lane. Several of the children I played with in the yard and at school lived here; they seemed much happier than the children in the main building. I was assured I would not have to see Miss Silverwood again.

Leaving me in my new surroundings, Auntie Agnes promised she would visit me on Tuesday after she had been to work. On her return,

I was able to share with her the good news that I liked where I was staying, but I missed Miss Green.

A few hours later, Miss Green appeared just before I was going to bed. She had met Agnes as she was about to go home. I will always remember Miss Green's little rotund body covered in a floral wrap-around pinafore, which emphasised her tyre-like curves. During the week, her snowy white hair often had in a few dinky curlers, partly covered with a silk head scarf depicting the royal coach and Union Jack. Come Sunday, the curlers were removed, revealing corkscrew curls framing her face. She had a beautiful smile, and occasionally a frowned look over the top of horn-rimmed glasses. Despite the large number of children she had to look after and the hard work involved, she never once showed violence or aggression towards any child. Even her clips around the ears, of which I got a few, were non-violent and painless.

Miss Silverwood was cunning enough not to inflict her vicious attacks on the children in front of other staff. It was her word against ours: children were seen and not heard! I am certain Miss Green and other members of staff feared Miss Silverwood. Staff did, however, see the outcome of the brutalities we endured. Miss Green did her best to save us from Miss Silverwood's onslaughts and she comforted us if we had suffered in her absence. She would have made a very good matron. Sadly, I never saw her again. I heard she had planned to leave residential work for pastures new.

My few meagre possessions were transferred from the locker room to my new abode. Here, I had a wardrobe, but clothing was still communal, so it remained empty. All my lovely manse clothes had disappeared. I had left my new rabbit with Auntie Agnes. The only things I could call my own were my now well-worn toothbrush, two pairs of shoes and my beret. (We were not allowed to wear other people's hats, but you could wear their knickers!) I also had my much-loved but well-used royal scrapbook.

This was a wonderful time to collect pictures of the royal family. I had amassed such a lot already. None were ever quite as spectacular as

Queen Elizabeth's Coronation Day pictures. A huge street party was organised for all the community, to which we were invited.

We were taken on a visit to the local cinema, where we watched the crowning of Queen Elizabeth on screen. In all my seven years, I had never seen such wonderful pageantry. It was always said that, if you visited our cinema, you went in wearing a cardigan and came out with a jumper! True to form, a few of us came out with something biting our legs and we ended the day covered in lashings of calamine lotion. Despite the itchiness acquired, we were so delighted to feel part of what proved to be a very caring community. At school, each child received a commemorative mug. As I rushed home with my new treasure, I turned a corner and tripped over a black Labrador dog. My knees were badly grazed, and my pride hurt, but my mug was intact!

Society was changing and we were soon to benefit from these changes. We were no longer seen as the 'bad kids'. Most people were demanding better ways of caring for children. They viewed the large Dickensian children's homes with scorn and contempt. The old expressions of 'orphans' or 'inmates' were banned from every-day usage. We were now to be known as residents in residential homes. However, some people still clung to the misguided thought that any child in a children's home must be there because they had done something wrong.

Even today, some misinformed people associate the words 'children's homes' with so-called 'bad kids'. As an adult, I was asked, 'What did you do wrong to grow up in the homes?'

I replied, 'Nothing, absolutely nothing.'

***

I was so fortunate to be in one of the first groups of children to leave Rothwell Cottage Children's Home – which was generally known locally as the orphanage – forever. Auntie Agnes ensured I was well informed of the intention to transfer me to another smaller family unit. Although I was a little apprehensive, I was also excited as the taxi appeared and a lady got out and walked to towards me. She put her hand in mine and said, 'Hello I'm Miss Smith, your new housemother, and I wouldn't be here if I wasn't Irish!'

Her very petite body was neatly dressed in a blue and white shirt-waister dress, the height of fashion at the time. Her fair hair had been carefully parted, waved at one side, and glistened in the late afternoon sun. There was a real air of gentleness about her, and yes, she had a lovely Irish accent. I instantly liked her. I was the first child to be collected. As the taxi passed through the black wrought-iron gates, I looked back at the Rothwell homes for the very last time. In years to come, the bulldozers moved in and cleared the site, but not the memories!

Other children were collected from various homes on the way. One boy was slightly older than I was. He chatted away as if we had known each other before. There was an emotional scene when we collected his twin brothers, who he had not seen for a few months. The reunion was rather special. Even the taxi driver allowed time for them all to hug each other.

A little girl with fair hair and a sad little face occupied the seat next to me. The child immediately cuddled into me. Her round-framed spectacles were far too big and kept slipping down her nose. I instantly like her, too.

The next child sat very quietly at the other side of me. She had beautiful thick brown hair. She also had a very sad look on her face and stared out of the window in silence for the entire journey.

We could not believe our eyes when we stopped outside a house in Raynel Drive, Ireland Wood, Cookridge, on the outskirts of Leeds. The house had been purpose built to blend in with the local housing. Inside there was a wonderful smell of newness. Every room was furnished with matching teak furniture. In the kitchen, new Formica work surfaces looked beautiful and modern. Even the china dishes in the kitchen cupboard were brand new and very pretty. There was not an enamel mug in sight. There were no heavy wooden bumpers, or huge tins of liquid wax polish.

Upstairs there were five bedrooms. Miss Smith's bedroom was at the front of the house; the boys shared the four-bedded room and a further two twin-bedded rooms were used by the younger girls. I could not believe my ears when Miss Smith announced I was to have the single bedroom at the end of the corridor. She explained this room had been designated as the isolation room, hence the white washbasin in one corner. I was told, should the room be required, I would have to exchange it with whoever was ill at the time. What would happen if a boy were sick? I sincerely hoped nobody would be sick! The view from the window looked out across the road to a newly built church and beyond to some rather old, but to my mind beautiful trees.

I was enthralled with everything I had seen in the house and, even more so, with the wide garden space outside. I could not believe this was a children's home. It was so comfortably furnished, and homely in every way. The next day, another brother and sister joined us. Their stay, however, was very short. Two more siblings took their place. I realised that brothers and sisters were now staying together. How I hoped Kevin and I would soon be reunited. Alas, it was not to be – all the vacancies had been filled.

The next day, Miss Smith took us all to a large warehouse in Leeds and brand-new outfits were purchased. Every child had some choice as to colour or style. On our return, we were delighted when we were allowed to store our new clothing in the wardrobes and drawers in our bedrooms. There was to be no more clothing that was communal and each child was to be treated as an individual.

Within weeks, we were like one big family. We were so happy under the care of Edna 'Ann' Smith, but we all still carried rather too much emotional baggage from earlier days. We often shared our experiences. It was clear that emotional scars of varying degrees lay just below the surface of each child's subconscious mind and would, from time to time, raise issues which Miss Smith and others would have to address. I heard some very sad accounts of neglect and abuse prior to their admission into care from some of the other children.

In this home, there were no arduous tasks, just a regular general cleaning routine. We were all expected to clean our rooms at least once a week. Miss Smith would only intervene if cleaning did not meet her high standards, but even then, she would lead by example and work alongside any who failed her scrutiny, thereby teaching us good practices.

One day, when Miss Smith was inspecting a boy's room, she saw a spider in its web hanging from the curtain rail. She said to the boy, 'Make sure you put a duster over that before I come back to inspect the room.' The next day she returned to find a yellow duster draped over the curtain rail; the dead spider was dangling precariously behind it!

We were encouraged to help prepare menus and cook meals. There were no special meals for the staff, as I had seen elsewhere. We all sat at the same table and ate the same kind of food. In every way, we were treated as equals. Miss Smith taught us how to repair any damaged garments, and how to safely change light bulbs. I was taught how to put up a new curtain pole in my bedroom, a valuable lesson for later life and one that gave me an interest in woodwork! Wastefulness was discouraged. On vacating a room, all lights and other electrical appliances had to be switched off and doors had to be closed to comply with fire regulations. Otherwise, no major rules applied. Common sense was expected and good behaviour was rewarded with praise and an occasional extra treat.

Large items of laundry, such as bedding and curtains, were sent away in wicker baskets to be cleaned, while personal clothing was washed in the laundry room. Each child was taught to how wash, iron and put away their own clothes and keep their wardrobes and drawers tidy. I found this easy compared to Rothwell's regime. There were no back-breaking tasks anywhere in this cleaning routine, but there was never any room for dirt or untidiness in Ann Smith's home! Her two mottos were: 'Cleanliness is next to Godliness' (we were very clean), and 'Remember, if everything is put away in its rightful place, it's easier to clean a room.' We remembered, and the house really did become a show home to the Leeds City dignitaries and other visitors who came from everywhere to see this new method of childcare.

Miss Cooper, another housemother, stayed with us for a few months until she took responsibility for another small residential home not far away. It was structurally identical to ours, but when we visited it, the different interior gave it its own character. We were all very sad to say goodbye to Miss Cooper as she had always been so kind to us. I remember her teaching me how to paint pictures in my colouring book. Her paintings were beautiful and left me inspired to look at other artworks.

★★★

One day, Miss Smith took two of us to Leeds railway station to collect a surprise parcel from Manchester. We were intrigued when a large old suitcase with holes in the top and sides was handed down from the luggage van. On closer inspection, inside, lying in cotton wool, was a tiny little black mongrel puppy. Imagine our joy when we were told it was ours to keep. My companion insisted he wanted to carry the puppy all the way home, but quickly changed his mind when it peed down his leg. I was highly amused and unafraid to carry this little creature home, puddles or no puddles.

Named Kim, this little dog was to bring us all such joy. There was never any shortage of dog walkers. Even the youngest child would take Kim to the local playing field and prepare his tea on his return. Often after Sunday lunch, Miss Smith would take us for walks in the surrounding area. A favourite walk of mine was to Adel Church, in a local historic village. Kim would always run alongside us until we reached the churchyard. Here, he was made to sit and wait until we had looked around the old building.

This lovely old church with its ornate Norman arched doorway and beautiful stained-glass windows fascinated me. Inside there was a real sense of peace. Miss Smith encouraged us to sit quietly and observe the carvings created over many years by stonemasons, whose labours had lasted many centuries.

I soon realised that if I offered to take Kim out after school, I could spend some time alone. I enjoyed the moments of quiet solitude in the lovely countryside. I began to look more closely at the world around me. I saw beauty in the trees around the church and the seasons brought their own colours. The daffodils in the church yard remined me it was spring and the woodland floors were carpeted with bluebells through which young rabbits scampered. I began to wonder who created such lovely things and puzzled over how creation started. I loved the beautiful wayside flowers and often returned with a bunch of flowers for Miss Smith. On one occasion, I really overstepped the mark and lifted a nice ready-made bunch from a grassy area, unaware at the time that this was an unmarked grave. I was promptly sent back and had to return the bouquet to its rightful owner, sadly no longer with us!

Miss Smith had a good level of kindly discipline. We had very few rules, but certain things were not tolerated without correction. One rule was that Kim was not allowed in the kitchen during the day. He did, however, sleep between the cooker range and the huge coke boiler at night, only to be evicted from his warm bed first thing in the morning.

Having spent a playful time with Kim in the garden one day, I came running into the kitchen with Kim hot on my heels. Miss Smith was busy making a chocolate cake. Seeing my misdemeanour, she shouted, 'Jesus, Mary and Joseph, behave yourself!' Cheekily, I asked her what Jesus, Mary and Joseph had done! She raised the wooden mixing spoon in the air and, as she did so, some of the chocolate cake mixture splashed onto my face. I laughed, and with my fingers began to lick off the delicious mixture as I was chased from the kitchen. Kim licked up a few drops from the floor. He too was hastily evicted. As the remaining cooked cake was passed around at teatime, I received a much smaller piece than everyone else did. A fitting punishment, discreetly administered!

Anyone who committed misdemeanours that were more serious was told that their name would be put in the black book, which was kept in the kitchen drawer. One day I was curious to know how often my name had been entered. When I opened the book, there was only one entry: a recipe for Yorkshire pudding!

Miss Smith had a gentleman friend called Stanley Meadows, who came to visit her most Tuesdays, which was her official rest day. Stanley was a vicar at a church in Manchester. He was a tall, handsome man with dark wavy hair. He was always full of fun and added to the home the fatherly touches – we were all very fond of him. Miss Smith and Stanley shared an old red car they called 'Jezebel'. Only two children could squeeze in the back seat. Occasionally, we had to get out and push when the engine suddenly cut out; this only added to our spirit of adventure.

As chaplain to the Territorial Army Parachute Reserves, Stanley had to do parachute practice and, during school holidays, we were taken in turns to an airfield to watch him jump. These were such special outings. I was given a ripcord off an old parachute as a memento of the day, which I proudly showed to my school friends. Stanley smoked a pipe, but at the same time taught us the dangers of smoking by asking us to hide his matches, which we frequently did. However, we would enter the room again and amidst smoke clouds discover he had used Miss Smith's cigarette lighter. Miss Smith knitted Stanley a smoking jacket, quite the fashion rage at the time. Stanley bought her a really smart cigarette holder, but it did not look quite right with Woodbines, so it stayed in the drawer.

***

Doris Dean, the friend of Agnes who I had first met on my visit to Leighton Buzzard, had sought permission to write to me on a regular basis. Her weekly letters were full of lovely details of her activities and Henry Dean, Doris's father, sent me seeds for the garden or cuttings of plants with the instructions regarding planting and aftercare.

A huge Bramley apple tree grew in their garden at Rothschild Road, Leighton Buzzard and so the Dean family sent large parcels of apples by rail, which we collected from the Parcels Office at Leeds Station. Miss Smith baked delicious pies and always reserved one for Auntie Agnes to take home when she came to take me out on Saturdays. We also received boxes containing prize chrysanthemums that Henry had grown. The flower stems were very carefully wrapped in wet tissue paper and each bloom protected with cotton wool. I loved arranging these flowers in vases, which were placed around the home. Doris also produced some beautiful knitted jumpers for all the girls and boys.

Auntie Agnes worked for a tailoring company in the centre of Leeds called Heaton's, which specialised in making coats. The owner very generously gave Agnes offcuts of quality materials, which she converted into skirts for the girls. Her tailoring skills were also used to professionally repair the holes in the boys' trousers.

★★★

Our first Christmas in Raynel Drive was very special. We had all been asked to send the 'Santa letter', but with a proviso that we could only ask for one small thing. I requested a doll with eyes that would open and close.

Before Christmas, the *Yorkshire Evening Post* ran knitted toy campaigns for needy children. I was the recipient of a gorgeous doll dressed in blue and white skiing clothes. Underneath its jumper was a letter from a lady named Gladys, who had created the outfit. I sent a thank-you letter, and received several letters from her although we never met.

I was most grateful for her gift and was saddened when I lost one of the doll's knitted bootees. I went to the local police station. Childlike, I hoped someone would find it and hand the bootee in. The police officer wrote down the details and description. A few days later, the police officer and his wife came to the home with two pairs of knitted dolls' bootees that the policeman's wife had knitted for me. Another grateful thank-you letter was sent.

I saw this same knitting pattern in a *Woman's Weekly* magazine and promised myself if ever I had a little girl, I would create the same doll's outfit for her. Unfortunately, I lost the pattern. Like most young girls, I was beginning to dream of a future with a real family of my own. These thoughts did sometimes lead me back to the subject of my mother's abandonment, and fears that I may not make a suitable mother because I reasoned I had no mother's example, but, as time passed by, I realised that all the single ladies who were having so much input into my life were the finest example of true motherhood I could ever know.

Excluding, of course, Miss Silverwood.

Out walking in Holbeck one day, a woman stopped and said, 'Hello. I'm Miss Silverwood.' Fearfully, I took hold of Auntie Agnes's hand. She squeezed my hand gently and, looking Miss Silverwood in the eye, said, 'We know who you are. Goodbye.'

Many months later, I was sitting by the fireside with Auntie Agnes, when she looked over the top of her newspaper and said, 'Do you know who has stopped taking sugar in her tea?' (an expression she used when reading the obituary column).

I looked up from my sewing and confirmed I didn't know.

'Miss Silverwood,' Agnes replied.

Fourteen

REAL CHILD WELFARE

A new senior care officer, Cyril Purnell, was employed with overall responsibility for implementing many of the new welfare changes in the Leeds area. He was a regular visitor to our home and was very popular with all the children. His approachable manner and good rapport with Miss Smith greatly enhanced the ease we felt in asking questions about our identities.

One day, I asked him where my father was. He delayed answering my question until I was taken into the sitting room and the door closed. Sitting beside Miss Smith, I listened to the account of my father's removal to prison. I was obviously very upset and asked what crime my father had committed. I was somewhat relieved when I heard he had not committed some horrendous crime but had failed to pay maintenance for me and repeatedly had not provided details of his whereabouts to the Labour Exchange. Although I would hear again of the same offence being committed and my father's subsequent short admissions to HMP, I never heard of any other causes for his imprisonment.

I never recall having any strong desire to trace my father. Perhaps this stemmed from the fact that I felt he had abandoned Kevin and me in Street Lane Reception Centre. I did, however, pray God would bless him.

I asked where Kevin was now. There seemed to be some reluctance to answer this question. I always came upon negativity at the very mention of Kevin's name, but I persisted with my questions. Eventually, I was advised my brother was no longer under the care of Leeds Social Services. Meetings were always hastily closed whenever I raised Kevin's name to such a degree I began to wonder if Kevin was still alive.

I now had a new social worker. Miss Glen came from Wales and she was a lovely bubbly person, with a great capacity for laughter. It was always a joy to see her. On each visit, copious notes would be written, none of which I was allowed to see or to know the contents of the file that was beginning to bulge at the seams. She often told me how beautiful the Welsh mountains were, adding that I should someday visit them.

Miss Glen helped me to realise that not all social workers wanted to harm me. It took a great deal of time and patience for the genuine ones to convince me they only had my welfare at heart. Miss Glen was different: I trusted her, and she never once let me down. I shared with her how in the past I easily became angry if I thought I was being constantly ruled by social workers who only appeared for brief unproductive (in my estimation) meetings. They seemed to have the power, even over my regular carers, to say yes or no to any requests. Miss Glen suggested that when I felt angry, I was to get a piece of paper and screw it up tight and throw it into the waste paper bucket with all my might. I often missed the bucket and others sadly caught more than the paper!

My experiences with violence and abuse had left me with some temper. Inwardly, after Miss Silverwood's last vicious onslaughts towards me, I vowed that I would never again allow myself to be subject to such aggression. I would retaliate with all the force I could muster against anyone who mistreated me. This vow was once tested when a trainee carer lifted a hairbrush with the intention of punishing me for some minor misbehaviour. I grabbed the brush out of her hand and pointed it towards her face. 'Don't you ever hit me!' I shouted.

At that moment, Miss Smith came to see what was happening. Sending the two of us to separate rooms, I was asked to give my account of events. I was warned never to threaten staff. Miss Smith told me she understood why I felt so angry and made it clear that I should not have been subjected to any such threat. The trainee had absolutely no right to threaten to hit me, and with a hairbrush! Leaving me, Miss Smith went to the trainee. Even through the closed door, I heard her severely reprimand her for lifting a hairbrush with the intent of hitting one of her residents. I heard Miss Smith say, 'All these children have suffered violence or abuse, but none will suffer under my roof.' The trainee left the following day. I had to help Miss Smith clean out the ground-floor staff bedroom, which the trainee had left in an appalling filthy state – punishment enough for any misdemeanour!

The next day, Miss Smith called me into the sitting room and asked me to share with her why I had felt the need to retaliate so fiercely. I told her about Miss Silverwood's violence. From her response, I realised she already knew my background history. I shared with her my vow never to be abused again. I also shared with her how the trainee's action had activated within me such a strong response. I felt as though my whole being had gone into overdrive. I was inwardly shaking, but outwardly set to attack and defend myself. I burst into tears.

This was the first time I had cried since coming to this new home and now the floodgates had opened. It was some time before I could be consoled. I was then able to tell Miss Smith how frightened I felt about the sudden rage within me and the lack of control I had over it. She tried to explain the 'flight and fight' mechanism that all humans have, and how what I had felt was possibly a sudden rush of adrenalin ready to stand and fight back. I was scared. Would this happen again?

★★★

There were obviously times when we did not have contact with the child welfare officer due to his heavy workload, but we were allowed to make appointments to see him if Miss Smith was unable to help us or special permissions required his signature. The question of guardianship for children in the care system is very complicated and often makes the decision process for each child very slow. So many factors, details and restrictions all play a part in the outcome. The signature of the most senior welfare officer or court judge has to be sought before major plans are implemented.

This procedure caused some delay before Auntie Agnes could take me out on a regular basis to her own home. However, her visits to our new home were allowed, and each Saturday she would plan some outing for me. These were wonderful days. Together, we travelled by train to places in the Yorkshire Dales. I was developing a deep love of open spaces and little villages.

I enjoyed our visits to York with its cream-coloured stone buildings, its historic minster and little cobbled, narrow streets. Sometimes we would go on a sail down the River Ouse. On other occasions, we would take the train to Harrogate and walk through the lovely Valley Gardens that grace the town centre. The highlight of the day would be afternoon tea at Betty's Café, with its speciality delicious cream cakes.

There were times when I would think back to the days spent at the manse with Auntie Marjorie and Uncle William. I realised how influential they had been in encouraging me to appreciate nature and beautiful things.

Auntie Agnes had so many friends, and through her I met so many kind and caring people. Gifts, usually of money or sweets, were often given to me. I was never allowed to keep all the gifts, but I was given first choice as to which gift I could keep for myself. Auntie Agnes, in her wisdom, then encouraged me to share the rest with the other children. Miss Smith soon adopted this same strategy in the home and gifts from visiting people were equally shared out so we all benefitted from the kindness shown to us.

On Sundays, I would go with the entire household to the Church of England across the road. Mr Tindall, the vicar, actively supported Miss Smith's efforts to create a comfortable environment for us.

When the congregation gave a monetary gift at Christmas time, it was unanimously decided that we would purchase some trees for our back garden. The local garden centre manager helped us select suitable specimens, which we planted ourselves.

Sadly, my tree was the only one to die. I had decided I would plant daffodil bulbs beneath it and Miss Smith's theory was that I might have dug too deep and damaged the taproot. We revisited the centre, and I was given a copper beech, which flourished, albeit slowly.

I loved gardening, despite my first disaster, and was often the first to volunteer to weed the flowerbeds. I learnt so much from Miss Smith's vast knowledge of botany. We all had regular pocket money, and I often spent mine on plants and seeds, especially nasturtiums that grew so quickly and gave a colourful display. I soon discovered we could eat them and quite enjoyed their peppery taste. I was not, however, pleased when I discovered they were also a gourmet delight for earwigs, which made large holes in the leaves. One nip from an earwig's pincer-like tail was warning enough to leave them alone!

★★★

Mr Purnell's signature eventually endorsed all the permissions for Auntie Agnes to continue to visit me. Once it was established that I was settled in Raynel Drive, I was allowed to spend weekends in her home. The fact that Auntie Agnes's home had been considered the best place for me to go to in the circumstances in which I had been removed from the brutalities of Miss Silverwood was, indeed, a great honour to her care and love for me. I am sure that first visit paved the way for all future visits. Miss Smith was given the power to decide how long these visits should last. By now, her relationship with Agnes had developed into a real friendship that benefitted me in every way.

I remember so well my first full weekend in Mario Street, Holbeck, in Leeds where Auntie Agnes lived. Her little back-to-back house, like most houses in the area, had been built 100 years before my arrival to house the industrial workers of the local factories and railway companies. Now, the area carried the stigma of being called the Leeds slums.

Agnes's house did not have an indoor toilet or a bathroom, but it was no slum inside. To me, it was the cosiest little home I had ever lived in. Here, I knew I was wanted and loved. At the end of the street was the Yorkshire Penny Bank where Uncle William had taken me to invest my money. Seeing it obviously aroused some memories, but Auntie Agnes addressed this issue by allowing me to share my thoughts with her. She assured me that the Legassicks had transferred to another church as Mrs Wilson had indicated. I was in no way to blame for their departure from Leeds; it had been very much a church matter. The manner in which the separation from the Legassicks had occurred had apparently shocked the whole congregation. Sharing my memories and thoughts with Auntie Agnes helped me to lay another childhood ghost to rest.

Together, we spent our first Saturday afternoon walking among the flowerbeds on Holbeck Moor. Leeds Parks Departments were well known for their beautiful floral displays, providing vast swathes of colour and some welcome relief to the tenants in the rows of back-to-back houses, many of which had poor and dismal outlooks. We seemed to be constantly stopping to talk to people. I was amazed how well known Auntie Agnes was in her neighbourhood. She had, after all, been born in the house she still lived in. In the coming months, I began to realise that my special foster aunt was a real, valued member of the community and greatly loved by so many people who sought her support and advice on many issues.

Auntie Agnes introduced me to her sister, called Eleanor, but known to everyone as Cissie. I instantly liked her. She was wearing a Salvation Army uniform. After tea, she put on a most fetching little bonnet with a large ribbon tied in a bow at one side. Her lovely dark brown eyes seemed to sparkle as she smiled at me. In her hand, she held copies of *The War Cry*, the Salvation Army weekly paper, and a collecting tin. She would be going around the local pubs selling the papers bearing the Christian message and collecting money for the poor and needy in the community. In years to come, I would hear that Auntie Cissie was

Myself, aged nine, and Aunt Cissie (Eleanor Lowe). A most wonderful caring friend, wearing her Salvation Army uniform. Picture taken in Mario Street. She carried this photo of us in her Bible until the day she died.

frequently asked to sing George Bennard's hymn, 'The Old Rugged Cross', and drunken men were often reduced to tears hearing her sweet voice. I would also learn that several men had put down their drinking tankards and changed their lifestyles following talks with Cissie. There was a wonderful gentleness about her. I was so proud to call her Auntie.

On Sunday afternoon, holding Auntie Cissie's hand, I was allowed to march with the Salvation Army Band along Dewsbury Road into Fox Terrace, where the Army Hall was situated. The hall was rather old and dilapidated in parts, but the atmosphere inside seemed so warm and friendly. Several poor-looking people came and spoke to me.

I soon realised that both my foster aunties were special people and highly respected. Like her sister, Cissie was well known for her good works to others. The two sisters were extremely discreet people, but those who were recipients of their support were eager to share with others the kindness of my aunties. A very poor, sad-looking woman sitting near me turned and said, 'Your Auntie Cissie saved me from the drink,' which she said was 'so bad ... so bad the drink.' I was not sure what this meant and so refused the cup of tea handed to me at the end of the service. I did, however, enjoy the biscuit. By the time I arrived back at the house, I was so thirsty I drank lots of water from Auntie Agnes's tap because I knew it was 'good'. To this day, the sound of the Salvation Army playing the hymn tune of 'Onward Christian Soldiers' evokes such happy memories of that first weekend spent with these two dear sisters.

Auntie Agnes was still a member of Beeston Hill Church. I was old enough now to know that she would want to attend her place of worship each Sunday. I had not entered the building since the separation from the Legassicks. I shared my feelings about church attendance with her — I did want to return to Sunday school, but feared my emotions would get the better of me. We agreed to visit the church the following Saturday when Agnes was rostered to arrange the flowers ready for the Sunday service.

When the day arrived, we walked to the church together. Most of the journey was uphill through long streets of terraced houses. Entering the building did feel rather strange, but there was no deacon in the vestibule and all the pews were empty. Auntie Agnes sat down in her pew. She signalled to me to sit where I had so often sat before. Bowing her head in prayer, she asked God's blessing upon the two of us. This simple act of reverence calmed my fears.

Very soon, I was helping to arrange the church flowers. We arranged a small posy of flowers for the table in the vestry. When I entered the room, there on the wall was a picture of Uncle William, along with photographs of previous ministers. Silently, I looked at his face which seemed to be looking straight back at me. The tears just flowed.

Taking me in her arms, Auntie Agnes said, 'Let's go and sit where Aunt Marjorie used to sit.' Sitting there, I was able to think back to the happier times I had known in this place of worship. Again, taking me into her arms, Agnes told me that this could now be my place to sit, if I wanted to return to the church.

Later that day, Auntie Agnes telephoned Miss Smith and asked if she could take me to church and permission was granted. The next day, I sat in Aunt Marjorie's seat surrounded by so many people I could call real friends. Behind us sat the Wilson family. Alan, now a little older, shook my hand and said, 'Hello lass. It's grand to see you.'

Fifteen

FLY THE CROW'S NEST

I had no fear during the weeks now and I had settled well into Ireland Wood Primary School. My first teacher, Miss Rhine, took a great deal of time in ensuring all her pupils wanted to produce good work. She had a real capacity to bring out the best in each child by constantly stimulating new and interesting topics, accompanied by setting the child a small task to complete. I was to look after a stick insect, which she had brought from Leeds University. Collecting grass and leaves for it gave me pleasure and a short skive from the classroom. Surprisingly, the insect lived in its bell jar for the whole term, much to my delight.

May Day was to be a very special day for us. Following the old English tradition, we had practised our maypole dancing for many weeks until we could weave the ribbons around the pole with such precision. In assembly, the teacher asked us to dress in our best clothes on Open Day. Girls were to wear a pretty dress and coloured ribbons in their hair.

Miss Rhine gave me a letter addressed to Miss Smith asking for her permission for me to receive a gift. Permission granted, Miss Rhine called me into the staff room and gave me a beautiful dress, neatly folded and wrapped in pink tissue paper. I was instructed not to tell my classmates where it had come from. I felt very special as I gaily danced around the maypole. I never forgot this act of kindness.

Miss Rhine was not the only teacher to show kindness, or whose attention I enjoyed. Mr Mitchell was the English and physical education teacher. He was so handsome. I am sure he was totally oblivious of my first crush, although he did hear me tell a playmate that I thought he was so 'dishy'. My Superman turned, smiled, winked and carried on calling the class to order. His wife and daughter, Anne visited the school on open days. I enjoyed playing in Anne's garden and was invited to their house for tea. By this time, my first crush had cooled; I had my eye on a boy nearer my own age who was also handsome.

★★★

I entered my last year at primary school with real trepidation. I had heard so many things said about the secondary modern school, West Park, which I was to attend next. It was so large and impersonal. It certainly lived up to many of the accounts, although it also had some things in its favour. The excellent sports facilities, science labs and domestic science kitchens were a credit to the designer. In these departments, good teachers brought out the best in any who were willing to try hard. In all these subjects I achieved marks higher than I thought possible.

However, one English and maths teacher left many children, including myself, hating the subjects due to his bullying and threatening methods. This teacher was known as 'Crow's Nest', simply because he sported a thick black beard, but only on his rather prominent chin. A great many children suffered psychologically and failed exams though his sheer lack of clear instruction and his fear tactics!

I incurred his wrath one day, largely through his own insensitivity. He knew I lived in care and was called an orphan, although I now knew I wasn't an orphan. He asked the class to raise their hand if they had any siblings. I looked round and every member of the class acknowledged having brothers or sisters. I too put up my hand. I had a brother, Kevin.

We then had to write about a day in the life of our brother or sister. What could I write? I had only one very sad day's memory and I certainly did not want to share this lasting memory of my brother with him or my classmates. I sat there and stared out of the window with nothing written in my book. Crow's Nest came and stood over me for what seemed such a long time. He then rushed up to his desk, scribbled on a piece of paper, which he thrust into my hand and in front of all the class told me to go to the headmaster's office. On the way, I looked at the note, which read, 'Cane for insubordination'. I was caned without any questions asked.

Playtime brought a barrage of questions and a lot of genuine care from friends, except for one bullying girl, who said, 'You deserved caning as you told a lie, stating you had a brother'. She repeatedly poked her finger in my chest in a threatening manner. I had had enough. I ploughed into the girl with such force and aggression and only pulled back after two teachers had intervened. One, of course, was Crow's Nest.

This time I was delighted; both the bully and I were caned together. She cried; I held back the tears. Leaving the headmaster's office, I shouted, 'At least I got caned this time for something, not like last time for nothing!' I marched off the school premises and straight home to Miss Smith, who promptly marched me back to school. Along the way, I gave a full description of what had taken place. Miss Smith listened in silence and I really thought I was not going to get any support, but I soon realised she was more than willing to support me.

I remained in the headmaster's office throughout the meeting to investigate the circumstances surrounding the events. The headmaster was firmly told I should never have been caned without a thorough investigation as to the first offence. I was told I deserved to be punished for my aggressive outburst, although Miss Smith did point out that the other girl had implied that I was lying when I was not, and I was due an apology from her before she left school at home time.

The girl was called to the office and apologised. I equally had to apologise for the hurt I had inflicted upon her. Miss Smith then insisted Mr Crow's Nest came to the office. I was instructed to wait in the corridor but could hear Miss Smith berating him for his lack of compassion and understanding. When the office door opened, I heard Miss Smith say, 'It's time the education system got rid of caning. It is cruel and only breeds violence.' Crow's Nest left with a rather red face.

There was never any happiness left for me with this teacher, even though he made what I considered half-hearted attempts to restore my confidence. I never liked him and therefore did not try hard at English or maths. The only consolation here was the good English foundation lessons I had been given in Mr Mitchell's classes in the primary school. Maths remained, for the rest of my school days, a weak subject.

The friendship between my fighting classmate and me blossomed, however. She became a regular visitor to the home, and I received invitations to her home. Eventually, I plucked up courage to tell her very briefly how Kevin and I were separated as little children. I held back the main family facts. We both made a pledge that day that we would never fight each other again. I enlarged the vow by declaring I would never hit another person – unless I was in extreme life-threatening circumstances, then woe betide them. Otherwise, I would always keep my hands by my side or in my pockets.

At home, I was taken aside and asked why I had not used my screwed-up paper strategy taught by Miss Glen, my social worker. I said I didn't have any paper other than my book. With a twinkle in her eyes, Miss Smith said in her lovely Irish accent, 'Jesus, Mary and Joseph, you should have thrown the book!'

Sixteen

My Father's Gift

My time in Raynel Drive was gradually drawing to its close. Children stayed in the homes only until the age of fifteen, when it was then expected we would start work and make our own way in life. The dilemma facing the social workers was where the young people should stay after care. Organisations such as Dr Barnardo's had developed farms where some of their residents, particularly boys, could go to live and work. Some young people were placed in service in large country houses, but this practice was gradually being phased out as estate owners wanted to choose their own staff.

Hostels were the main options opened to Leeds children. These establishments were not the ideal places for young vulnerable teenagers who were leaving the protection of the children's homes, hence the reason for so many literally falling by the wayside. The Salvation Army or other denominations ran many of the hostels and most also housed alcoholic and society dropouts.

I was aware that Miss Smith and the social workers were looking at all the options open to me. I was taught as many life skills as possible in my teenage years, but I knew a hard road lay ahead. The authorities did still have some input until the age of eighteen and, occasionally, this extended to twenty-one, but resources were limited and social workers so thin on the ground. I knew that once I was no longer living in care, I would be alone against whatever came my way.

Miss Glen, my social worker, had moved to another district and had a new caseload. I missed her visits and her friendliness. My new social worker, Miss Foster, made arrangements for me to visit headquarters to meet her for the first time. In very sharp contrast to my previous social worker, Miss Foster had a very serious outlook on life. Everything was done by the book with no flexibility and little conversation. I struggled to formulate a like or dislike. I couldn't get to know her well enough to say I liked her, but at the same time there was nothing in her demeanour that caused me to dislike her. In the coming months we ambled along together, fulfilling the necessary statutory obligations.

I asked why I couldn't go and live with Auntie Agnes and was told she was technically too old (she was now sixty-five and retired) and also single, which barred her from applying to foster me. It seemed everything was stacked against me, until I personally asked Auntie Agnes if she would let me live with her. I had a resounding answer, 'Yes, of course you can if the authorities will allow the move.' I quickly asked for an appointment to see the welfare officer, but the wheels of decision making rumbled on for several months; I also had to attend two medicals and various meetings before any final decision was made.

During one of these meetings, the conversations came to a sudden halt, as was Miss Foster's habit. I looked down at my open file. Although it was upside down, I was able to read the name 'Mabel Ellis'. At the top of the same document were two initials and the name of a foster parent. I knew the name was not anyone connected to me, so I presumed it must have some connection to Kevin. I came away from the office elated and asked the bus driver if he could give me pen and paper to write down some important names I had to remember.

I finally had names – now I had to solve the mystery people. Alone in my room that night, I gradually worked out that one of these names could be my mother's maiden name. If so, it would also be the name of my maternal grandparents.

★★★

One day, while I was waiting for a decision, I was asked by Miss Smith to clean out some cupboards in her bedroom. I had never been asked to do this before. On the shelf was a large *Girls' Annual*. Being an ardent reader at the time, I opened the book. I was totally stunned when I turned the cover of the book and found there, written in what I discovered was my father's handwriting, a letter telling me he loved me and missed me so much. He hoped I would receive the Christmas present and write to the address at the top of the page.

I flew down the stairs and somewhat angrily turned on Miss Smith for withholding this valuable family gift. How much it would have meant to me all these years to know my father really did have some feelings towards me! For days, I sobbed my heart out. I was so distressed and deeply saddened. Why had the book remained in the cupboard all this time? No explanation was given to me then as to why the present had been secreted away. I had never before had any reason to mistrust Miss Smith, now I doubted her.

All of the cupboards throughout the house were cleaned out every six months as a matter of routine. Why, I reasoned, would this cupboard not receive the same cleaning regime when Miss Smith was so particular, and this was in her own bedroom? How could the book have laid unopened for so long? I felt utterly betrayed by someone who had shown me such kindness and who had been such a great friend and adviser.

Miss Smith had always supported me in real times of need; she had so often comforted me in distress. Now I mentally pushed aside all her efforts to console me. As far as I was concerned, there was no clear explanation to offer.

However, there was an address at the top of the page, and I memorised it before putting the book back in the cupboard as requested. Why I had to replace what was rightfully mine in the cupboard again baffled me. I was later unable to retrieve it because it was in Miss Smith's private room. Her room was never locked, but I had the respect she had so often taught us to ask before entering other people's rooms or touching their posessions. Somehow, I held onto that respect and did not go into the cupboard again, although I felt as if the only possession I had from my father had now been ravaged with time, and no true respect had been given to me or to my father regarding his gift.

Years later, I heard the sad news that Miss Smith was in the Ida Hospital, in Cookridge, with lung cancer. I made the journey to see her on my own. We talked openly about the book. I heard how it had arrived the first Christmas I had spent at Raynel Drive, and how she had sought the advice of her seniors at Social Services headquarters. They had instructed her to destroy the book and say no more about it to me. Feeling that this was deceitful, Miss Smith had put the book into her own cupboard. Time had passed before my discovery, which was purely by accident. Miss Smith had only wanted help cleaning her room as she was tiring very easily, and I always like tidying out cupboards.

She admitted she felt utterly devastated by my discovery and fully understood my reaction to her. There was no doubt, until this incident, I had held Miss Smith in very high esteem. She had a great love for each child in her care, and none were ever mistreated or abused in her home. I really struggled with my emotions after finding my father's gift, but I also loved Ann Smith. Hearing the true account of why the book had been withheld from me, I realised she was not to blame.

That day, we were reconciled to each other. As we parted, she said to me, as she had done many times before, 'Away and go kiss the Blarney Stone; it's like life, hard to kiss but well worth the effort.'

Leaving residential work behind, Ann Smith joined Stanley Meadows in Manchester, and later died in the arms of the man she loved. I wonder if she is still telling Jesus, Mary and Joseph to behave themselves in her lovely Irish brogue?

Seventeen

THE DEANS OF
LEIGHTON BUZZARD

Auntie Agnes had obtained permission for me to spend the school holidays with her. I was amazed how many consent forms she had to sign accepting total responsibility for my care. I barely understood the implications of caring for another person's child. It is only now, as an adult, I realise the tremendous pressure this must have put upon her.

I was offered the choice of two weeks at the seaside, or a holiday with the Dean family – the seaside lost the competition. I had previously enjoyed several wonderful holidays with Doris and her father, Henry Dean. Now, as they greeted us at Leighton Buzzard Station, I eagerly looked forward to our time together knowing this holiday would be very special, and at the end of it, I would not be returning to the children's homes.

The Dean family lived in a lovely red-bricked house in Rothschild Road, Linslade. The aroma of steak and kidney suet pudding gently steaming away on the old cooking range evoked memories of previous visits. Auntie Doris had been a cook in service, and her skills were perfected down to a fine art. Her brother, Reginald, was a master butcher and provided her with good cuts of meat. Despite every effort to teach me how to make such delicious dishes, cakes and pies, to my mind, nothing I have made equals her standard and taste. Teenagers are such hungry beings; I was so often described as having hollow legs as I packed away such good food.

I spent several days helping Henry in the garden. He was a lovely man with an irrepressible sense of humour. He had quite a portly abdomen, which seemed to be perched on two rather skinny legs, indicating he had possibly been much thinner at one time. His face was weather-beaten by years of outdoor work as a post office engineer and a long retirement in the veg plot!

I loved being in his company. One day I said, 'I wish you were my father.' Taking me into his arms, he said, 'You can call me Dad Dean.' Hearing these words brought a real sense of warmth into my whole being. I experienced such a surge of love for this dear old gentleman. His beautiful deep-set blue eyes twinkled beneath the thick, white bushy eyebrows. He kissed me, and his neatly trimmed moustache brushed away the tear that had trickled down my cheek. For the first time in my life, I felt I was at last someone's daughter.

Thereafter, Dad Dean was his name. He certainly lived up to being a true father figure to me. He shared with me the sorrow he had known in life, having lost some of his children to tuberculosis. His younger son, Les, only just survived but still suffered from chest problems.

Not all Henry's stories were sad. He had reached the age when the same story is repeated with such regularity and clarity that the listener can almost enter into the spirit of the event. One such story was the premature birth of Doris. Weighing in at only two pounds in the middle of the night, her arrival had caused some panic in the household. The midwife did not think the baby would survive and placed her in her father's arms while she attended her mother.

Henry was determined he would do everything he could for his child and sat up for forty-eight hours nursing the tiny bundle. Without a bottle for the baby's milk, he cleaned a leather glove and pierced a small hole in one finger through which the baby could suck milk.

Mother and baby survived, and Henry delighted in telling others, 'Doris is my two-pound bag of sugar and she is still as sweet as when she was born.' His philosophy now was to enjoy every minute of every day. 'Why worry about tomorrow,' he would say, 'The sun might shine, if we are lucky, but I would rather it rained so I don't have to carry the heavy watering can!'

We spent so many happy hours together. I shared with him my memories of Kevin and my strong desire to be reunited with him. Dad Dean listened and then said, 'Follow your dream with prayer and action.'

Each morning at precisely ten o'clock, Dad Dean would set out for his morning stroll around the local area. At eleven, he would return home and tell Doris which ladies he had met along the way. There was no doubt that Henry Dean was loved by many in the town. Doris would listen to his accounts of hugs and kisses, then hug him and tell him he was just a lovable old rascal and remind him his half a pint of beer and cheese sandwich was on the table. He would then sit contentedly reading his paper and smoking his pipe until lunchtime.

One day, when he was unable to light the tobacco, he jovially asked his daughter to place a poultice on his neck to draw up his pipe. Doris disappeared into the kitchen and made up a hot poultice. 'O Doris,' he said, 'I'm only kidding!'

'Well,' said Doris, 'for years, you have told me to do as I am told.'

At the side of the long garden, rows of sweet peas were carefully ringed on cane supports. Their perfume was wonderful, especially if the dew was still on them. I was promised that if I could find one pure yellow sweet pea among all the mixed colours, I would be given a pound note. For non-gardeners, this was virtually impossible at the time before hybrid development, so the chances of Dad Dean losing his pound were indeed slim. However, each morning I would go out and search for the elusive yellow sweet pea.

These were not the only peas growing there. There were peas for the pot. Dad Dean and I would hold the pea pods up to the sun and count the number of peas inside. Some peas would find their way into all four hollow legs, two of which were much older than mine! Doris would shout from the open window, 'If you eat them now, you'll have none for dinner!' Enough peas would usually return for the lunch, and a neighbour would swap some for an alternative veg from her garden.

The meal table was not the only source of good things. The canal side was a rich larder of developing hazel nuts (known locally as 'filberts'), which Dad Dean promised he would collect and post to us about Christmas time. There were wild raspberries and sweet blackberries, which we collected in abundance and turned into jam. Sometimes, we would stop and speak to the owners of the highly decorated barges moored along the water's edge. One owner offered us a trip to the locks a few miles along the canal in exchange for a basket of blackberries.

Dad Dean and I spent one memorable afternoon at the open-air market held in the High Street. The stallholders were often colourful characters with interesting stories to tell. Many came from outlying villages and sold vegetables and flowers that they had grown on their own small market gardens. We bought a bunch of flowers to take back to my two aunties, who had stayed at home – no doubt enjoying a much-needed rest!

An old, well-used bicycle was resurrected from the shed. Horace, Auntie Doris's second brother, gave me a few cycling lessons. After a good few tumbles, I was on my way to becoming a more proficient cyclist and would ride alongside Doris. We visited Old Linslade Cemetery with flowers for her mother's grave, then called at the little teashop in the High Street and enjoyed an afternoon tea before returning home.

As we cycled along the lovely country lanes, I began to realise that if I had a bicycle at Auntie Agnes's home, I would have the freedom to search for the address on the inside page of my father's Christmas book. It had already dawned upon me if the book had been sent directly from my father, then he must have been aware I lived in Raynel Drive. This obviously raised its own questions as to why he had not visited in person. I was unable to answer the question myself and, like so many mysteries, it lay unsolved for now.

Dad Dean's second son, Horace, and his daughter, Valerie, and I spent a memorable day at Whipsnade Zoo, where a disgruntled camel spat in my face. On another occasion, Auntie Agnes and I received an invitation to join the domino and horticultural clubs on their annual trip to Windsor. What wonderful pictures I could have added to my Rothwell scrapbook but sadly it, like other childhood items, had passed from my hands to others along life's way.

I was rather sad when this holiday ended and I realised how much I loved the Deans of Leighton Buzzard. However, It was now time to return with Auntie Agnes to Mario Street and the start of life outside the children's home. These were indeed halcyon days.

Eighteen

BEYOND ALL UNDERSTANDING

All the consents and necessary documents required for me to transfer to the care of Agnes Lowe were completed. I had very mixed feelings when the day came for me to say goodbye to Miss Smith and the loving and caring environment I had known in Raynel Drive. I was naturally saddened to leave all the other children, knowing that once we parted I would never be allowed to return. Social Services had already assigned my bed to another child, who was arriving later that day. Arrangements were made for me to transfer to Auntie Agnes's home prior to the start of the new school term.

Until now, I had shared Auntie Agnes's big double bed and I had loved the cosiness of having her near me on my weekend visits. Now, the authorities decided that twin beds were more desirable. On this occasion, they were right. I was a young, rapidly developing teenager, requiring my own space.

Our new beds were most comfortable, but now Auntie Agnes had nowhere to hide her money! The brass knobs on the four posts of the old bed all screwed off and the rent, coal and food money were stored in the knobs until payments were due.

This lovely old bed had been purchased by my aunt's parents prior to their marriage. It had been the birthplace for Agnes and Cissie, and a real refuge for me from the violent abuse of Miss Silverwood. The old bed, along with all the double bed linen, was given to a family of nine children who lived down Mario Street. I later learnt that seven children were sleeping in the bed top to tail, or 'pigging', as it was known in Yorkshire. I wondered how long the already-sagging springs would last under the strain.

We may have had twin beds, but there was only one large bedroom and a very small room for Auntie Cissie, who by now had retired and come home to live. I had the use of the beautiful mahogany wardrobe and dressing table, both of which had large mirrors reflecting light around the room. Agnes had a smaller combined wardrobe and drawers.

There was little room for anything else, except the small black fire grate with its chimney stuffed with newspaper to keep out the draughts. Nothing else was needed. Everything was stored away neatly in its place, and the room dusted on a daily basis.

On the landing there was a threepenny-bit-shaped commode with a highly polished lid and a constant smell of Dettol or Three Hands disinfectant emanating from it. This was only used for night-time emergencies as the toilet was in the midden, or privy, three doors down the street. Here, newspapers were cut into little squares and threaded onto a piece of string that hung on the back of the toilet doors. On summer nights, you could sit there and read the latest news; in winter, you hurried in and out quickly! If the family was financially flush, you had IZAL toilet paper, which was usually stored in the house, or perhaps a few squares in your pocket. Each week, one household would scrub out the toilet, sweep the passageway and disinfect the midden (dustbin) area. I never saw a dirty toilet in our area. Living in such tight communities, neighbours had to get along together. Fortunately, I never witnessed any disagreements in Mario Street.

The doors of some houses were on street level. At our end of the cobbled street, you entered the house via three well-worn and frequently scrubbed steps. There was great pride among the local women and those who could afford white or sandstone created a line along the edges of the steps. They would also polish the brass door snecks (latches) until they glistened. The flagstones outside the house were swept daily and swilled down regularly with buckets of water.

Like all the houses in Mario Street, our house had only one room downstairs. One corner was designated for the kitchen area, where an old, brown stone sink with a shining brass tap provided the only daily washing facility – for bodies and dishes! A pretty chintz curtain was wired across the corner, providing some privacy. An enamel jug full of water was permanently placed in the fire-range oven and provided our only source of hot water, other than the cast-iron kettle with a glass marble inside that rattled and rolled, letting us know the water was near boiling point. I soon realised how well equipped the home in Raynel Drive had been in comparison to all the work my aunts had to do, especially on washday.

Very few houses in the area had running hot water. Most householders had to fill Peggy tubs from water that was heated on the fire range. This meant an early start lighting fires and filling large pans of water on washdays. Washing hung on lines across the streets and anything from blankets to bloomers fluttered in the breeze.

The table was covered in thick pieces of blanket, covered with an old piece of sheeting that was used for ironing. There was no spare money available to buy an electric iron. Ours was a black iron, called a flat iron, that was placed in front of the fire to heat. After a few minutes, you spat on the iron and, if the saliva sizzled away, you knew it was hot enough to use.

If your neighbour was out and it rained, you rushed out to bring in your washing and theirs. Often neighbours would call to collect their washing and find it on a wooden clothes horse, drying for them around a blazing coal fire. I saw a few occasions when my two aunts ironed the items too, especially if they belonged to some old person or a mother with a house full of children. There was never any financial charge for these acts of kindness. Sometimes there would be a knock at the door and some small child would say, 'Miss Lowe, Mummy said thank you for the washing, and if you want any errands run, I will go for you for nowt.' The child usually went away with a sweetie popped into their mouth by one or other of the Miss Lowes.

Beside the sink stood a very small gas cooker; its trade name, 'New World', barely reflected modernity, but it was the pride of the home. It was a speedier way to cook than the range, especially on hot summer days. However, there was no better oven for Auntie Agnes's delicious stew and dumplings than the coal-fired oven. On winter evenings, we often ate hot toast made in front of the blazing fire with lashings of Yorkshire butter and a little homemade jam.

The fireplace, with its high mantelpiece and attractive highly polished chrome fittings, was black-leaded every week with Zebrite, a liquid applied with a brush and burnished to a shine with a cloth and elbow grease. The furniture was beeswaxed and the lino on the floor was swept daily and scrubbed regularly. The two rag rugs were lifted and taken into the street and beaten with a cane beater. The bedroom carpets were 'Ewbanked' (a carpet sweeper) daily.

If all this sounded like drudgery, it really wasn't; it was accepted as the daily cleaning routine of most households at the time. Much of this work was carried out while I was at school, but I did enjoy taking my share at weekends.

A very old, but well-maintained treadle Singer sewing machine stood in one corner of the room. I now realised how difficult it must have been for Agnes to make so many lovely garments for me in such a small space, and I was not the only recipient of her needlework – neighbours often brought items for repair or alteration. This unpaid labour clothed many a child in the area.

Below the room, the whitewashed cellars were used for storage of meat, milk and butter, carefully wrapped in muslin or covered with stoneware covers that were soaked in water for extra cooling. The coal was also kept down there, separated from the food tables or cabinets by a wooden door. When the coalman came, it took considerable time for the coal dust to settle after he had emptied twenty hundredweight bags, or one ton of coal, down the chute ready for the winter months. The coalman would collect the carefully saved payment, then return half a crown for Cissie to put in her collecting tin. The milkman came every Friday to collect his money for the seven-day milk delivery. He too left a donation, knowing that Cissie would be visiting the market to gather fruit and vegetables for some poor recipient in the community. Although the rent man had to collect the full rent, he often brought a cake for me!

★★★

It was into this lovely home I came with all my possessions. The joy and comfort were already known to me, but now I had the most important human needs of all: security, stability and unconditional love. What more could a growing young girl want? These were wonderful days.

I thought I was free from the constraints of life under constant authoritarian rule and committee decisions, but I soon discovered I was still under their thumb. Poor Auntie Agnes had to seek the committee's consent for any activity I wanted to join in away from her home. Visits outside Leeds' boundary were rigorously vetted and letters of consent passed back and forth between our home and Social Services' headquarters.

Prior to my transfer to this lovely peaceful home, Auntie Agnes had to sign forms agreeing to abide by certain rules and regulations regarding my upbringing. One rule was that I must attend a Christian place of worship. This was no trouble at all to Auntie Agnes, as she had been a member of the local Baptist church for many years, and Auntie Cissie was a member of the Salvation Army. I loved going to the two different places of worship and, over time, made several friends at both places.

At the church, I was offered a part in the Christmas nativity play as the angel Gabriel. Throughout the rehearsals, I was constantly reminded to speak louder so the people at the back of the church could hear me.

The day of the performance arrived with a flurry of excitement. It was the practice of this church to keep photographs of previous ministers on the vestry wall. I was to change into my angelic costume in the vestry, but, 'I cannot change there with the photograph of the Reverend W.G. Legassick [Uncle William] staring at me!' I protested. Someone turned his picture to the wall.

After the service, a member of the congregation complimented me on my loud voice, saying he thought even the real angel Gabriel would have heard it! Returning to the vestry, I turned Uncle's photograph back again and, looking directly into his photographic eyes, I said, 'Here I am – an angel at last.'

As I took off my white robes and tinsel-covered wire halo, I paused in thought. I realised I was not very angelic because I still harboured feelings of anger and rejection. Inwardly, I struggled to accept the Social Services' system, although deep down I knew that without such places as children's homes, life for myself and many more children would have been horrendous. In Rothwell, I had known brutal treatment at the hands of one so-called carer, but I had also known people who were totally dedicated to my well-being and had provided me with love beyond measure.

A few weeks after the nativity play and during the evening service, the following hymn was sung by the church choir:

> Just as I am, without one plea,
> But that Thy blood was shed for me,
> And that thou bidsts me come to Thee,
> O Lamb of God I come.

(Charlotte Elliott 1789–1871)

I can barely describe the feeling of warmth that came over me. It was like being bathed in warm springs. I wanted the beautiful feeling to last forever. I knew I was no angel! I did, however, want to be a better person. I also knew that my Unseen Guest, my childhood name for Jesus, was personally very real to me.

At the end of the service, I went to the minister and asked to be baptised into the church membership, immersion in water being the symbolic way that Baptists show their acceptance of Christ as their Saviour. I was horrified to learn that even Reverend McLean had to obtain the Social Work Committee's approval to baptise me.

I felt so frustrated; to me, this was an infringement of my rights to choose my own place of worship. I struggled with very rebellious feelings – so much for feeling angelic! I reasoned that my relationship with my Creator was very personal to me. I required no one's permission to be a believer in Jesus Christ, or to confess that belief openly in baptism.

I had obviously had examples of good Christians around me and, from early days, had attended various denominations, but I had never been indoctrinated or forced to choose in whom I believed. I think these feelings were well summed up in a poem I wrote at the time, which I hope clarifies my own faltering steps into Christian faith:

My Unseen Guest

Sometimes I walk in a dark ravine,
But not alone, with the One unseen;
My faltering steps He guides,
And every need supplies.
I know His hand rests on me,
Even though His hand I cannot see.

Sometimes I walk in pastures green,
But not alone, with the One unseen.
Revitalised the soul aspires,
Strengthened to face the darkest hours,
And I feel His hand on me,
Even though that hand I cannot see.

Eventually, after several interviews at Social Services headquarters, permission was granted. I became a church member.

Nineteen

BROKEN BONES
AND AEROPLANES

On my first day at Hillside School for Girls, Mrs Fletcher introduced me to her well-established class. All the girls seemed very friendly but curious as to why I lived with an old lady. I had never thought of Auntie Agnes as old! A simple explanation had been given to the class that I had no parents. I knew this was not strictly true, but it was how others would view the situation. I was to be treated with respect, and no emphasis put on the fact that I was any different from anyone else in the class. All the girls were very kind to me. Within a few weeks of being at the school, I was accepted into the hockey and netball teams, much to my delight.

The excellent teaching skills of Mrs Sanderson and Mrs Fletcher resulted in improved school reports by the end of the first year, much to my two foster aunties' pride and my own. My English results were higher than expected and maths was still very much in the lower levels, but sports had produced its own silver cup for discus throwing. At last, the muscles of bumper polishing days had been put to better use!

Domestic science was taught in a house at the top of Beeston Hill. Here, cleaning rooms and preparing meals was part of the school curriculum. This lesson proved such a doddle for one who had scrubbed and polished twelve- and sixteen-bedded dormitories in the bleakness of early life. Sadly, our first delightful domestic science teacher had left by the second term. Her replacement was a person with the foulest mouth I had ever heard on educational premises. Our class heard of her reputation in the school playground and, even there, our informers used abbreviations of her words. We dreaded our first lesson.

However, I was not to be in this teacher's class for some time due to an accident in the gymnasium. I had been selected for a high jump competition and was being coached by Mrs Fletcher. I jumped over the bar and landed on my knee on a rather thin mat (these were standard at the time). The pain in my knee was excruciating. At the precise moment of the accident, the fire alarm sounded. Instructing the girls to assist me, Mrs Fletcher left to attend to her fire duties. The headmistress, Miss Beresford, passed us at the door and told me move along quickly, saying, 'You've only knocked your shin, girl! Hurry up get out of the building.'

Crying and in severe pain, I hobbled out of the door and sat on the school wall. It was now dinner time, and after rollcall all the girls were dismissed. In the meantime, I was left to my own devices as most of the local girls like me went home for lunch. I tried to walk home but didn't get very far before my knee doubled in size. Unable to go further, I sat on another wall. Realising that I was late home, Auntie Agnes came looking for me. As soon as she saw my condition, she ran along the road to the telephone box (mobiles, of course, hadn't yet been invented) and called the ambulance.

At the hospital, I was diagnosed with a dislocated patella (kneecap) and a piece of chipped bone, and surgery was needed. Hours passed, and there seemed to be so much confusion as to who could sign the surgical consent form. Apparently, Agnes was not authorised to sign the form as she was officially unrelated to me, even though she had known and cared for me longer than anyone else. The duty social worker was out of telephone range and not due back in the office for three hours. Theatre staff were on standby, but could not proceed without someone's signature, and all the while I lay there in what I can only describe as agony.

The appalling delay in obtaining a speedy consent signature was difficult to understand. I strongly resented the fact that when the duty officer eventually arrived she never came to see me, and yet she was able to intervene where Agnes could not. In hindsight (which is a wonderful teacher), the duty officer probably had her own caseload pressures before receiving the message about me. However, as an injured child, I had no comprehension of such matters at the time; relief from pain was all I craved. At seven o'clock in the evening, I was finally taken to theatre.

Throughout all this delay, Auntie Agnes had sat patiently with me and wiped away my tears. Knowing the household routine at home when coffee was served at ten o'clock each morning, the chances were she had had nothing to eat or drink since finding me on the wall, a long time for her to be without any refreshments. As always, she was uncomplaining of her own needs, but vocal about the time I was left waiting for relief.

No bed could be found for me, so I was taken home by ambulance in the early hours of the morning. I was laid on the Victorian horse-hair chaise longue, where I spent the rest of the night. Throughout the long hours, Auntie Agnes sat by my side, rising only to stoke the fire and make us both a cup of tea. I felt so comforted by her presence and gentle care. How different this was from the loneliness I felt when left alone in the isolation room in Rothwell with no one to comfort me

I was off school for six weeks, which I hated as I had always loved learning new things. The physiotherapist suggested I borrow a bicycle to exercise the knee joint, but the only one I knew of was the old rickety one I had used in Leighton Buzzard, miles away from Holbeck.

My gymnastic teacher, Mrs Fletcher, visited me at home. She was so upset, thinking she had neglected me. I assured her I fully understood the unprecedented circumstances she had faced at the time of the accident. I felt no anger towards her and it had been a genuine mistake.

During the next few weeks, the postman was a regular visitor, delivering get-well wishes. My school friends sent me cards, flowers and chocolates. I had not realised how many good friends I had through the church and school.

***

A few weeks prior to my accident, a letter had arrived from Uncle William and Aunt Marjorie inviting me and a companion of my choice to visit them in Jersey, where they now lived. Obviously, the letter had to go to headquarters. The response I received from the committee astounded me – I was to make the decision myself. The committee would sanction the visit only if I accepted the invitation.

The invitation caused my aunties untold stress. However, their openness and honesty prevailed and nothing was said to influence me either way. The adventurous part of the holiday, flying for the first time, appealed to me. Auntie Cissie definitely wanted to keep her feet on the ground, whereas it had always been an ambition of Agnes to fly. Auntie Agnes was the one person who would understand my fears and uncertainty.

I decided to visit Auntie Marjorie and Uncle William.

Eventually the consents were in order. I had resigned myself to enjoy the reunion and remember all the good times I had known with the Legassicks. Our coach and plane tickets arrived, amidst great excitement. Once more, the old treadle sewing machine trundled away as several new dresses were made. This time, I was able to help with the sewing, having had such a good teacher in Agnes.

Every morning, our sewing or any other activity ceased at ten o'clock, and everyone in the house would sit around the radio with our coffee and listen to the church service broadcast from Langham Place in London. After the service, one of my aunts would read a short passage from the Bible, say a prayer and withdraw a small scroll of paper on which was printed a Bible text from a little well-worn box, known as the Promise Box.

Throughout this morning's prayer time, I was acutely aware that something was troubling my aunts. It turned out that, due to a hospital appointment for physiotherapy, it seemed the holiday plans might be cancelled. No other dates for our trip were available as uncle had scheduled church commitments. However, the physiotherapist certainly worked hard on me in the meantime and I, in turn, ensured that all exercises were carried out with great gusto.

Twenty

PINK ELEPHANTS ON WHITE CLOUDS

We arrived at Manchester Airport in the early hours of the morning, ready for our scheduled flight. Once we were airborne the joy of seeing above the clouds was wonderful. The sun was shining over Jersey and we could see the whole island from the air.

To say I was apprehensive was an understatement and I sensed the same in Auntie Agnes. However, our fears were soon allayed as we ceremoniously shook hands with Uncle William and Auntie Marjorie, who reached forward to kiss me. They had naturally aged with the passing of time. There was still the same gentleness about them, still the same loveliness in Marjorie's face, and the same ministerial dog collar sitting comfortably around Uncle's neck. It was a squeeze getting our rather large suitcase and two extra passengers into the little grey Morris Minor.

The manse at Mont Millais, St Helier, on Jersey was vastly different from the manse in Leeds. Here, the thirties-style building was large and beautiful. The walled garden at the back was a blaze of colourful flowers and the outdoor table had been laid for morning coffee.

Our two bedrooms were at the back of the house overlooking the lovely garden. There was no blue silk eiderdown, as I had once known;

instead, a floral pink one covered the bed in my room. Drawer and wardrobe space had been made available to us and in the wardrobe hung the dress Auntie Agnes had made for me from the material decorated with the pink elephants on white clouds. I had so often wondered over the years what had become of this little dress, and here it was with all its memories, still hanging on its silk-covered coat hanger on a faraway island. I caressed it before hanging it back in its place and closing the wardrobe doors. Alone, later that night, I took the little dress out of its resting place and tearfully admired Auntie Agnes's wonderfully neat needlework. I thought of the day when I was just six years old and had worn this dress with such pride and joy.

Every effort was made to ensure our holiday was memorable. Outings to many interesting places around the island were arranged and garden tea parties were attended. I was uncertain of my feelings when Uncle William insisted on introducing me as his adopted daughter, which raised a few eyebrows!

The Legassicks were friends of Gerald Durrell, the great conservationist, who owned a small zoo on the island. We spent a lovely afternoon seeing his animal collection and were given a private viewing of some of the areas usually not open to the public.

I was allowed to use Auntie Marjorie's bicycle and was given a small map of the island. The ride to St Catherine's Bay gave me a wonderful sense of freedom. I telephoned the manse, as requested, to let them know I had cycled safely there and amazed everyone with how quickly I had arrived. The bright yellow gorse bushes on the cliffs looked stunning against the deep ultramarine sea. Taking a rest before returning, I was amused to see a farmer mixing large quantities of overripe tomatoes into cattle feed. I wondered if their milk would turn to red!

I enjoyed the tremendous beauty and freedom of the island. However, psychologically, things were far from comfortable. There were so many questions asked about the intervening years, but no explanation was given as to why the visits to Cranbrook Avenue came to such an abrupt end. In my mind, I desperately wanted to turn back the clock and be the adopted daughter. The little dress in the wardrobe was a constant reminder of early childhood days as the manse child.

There were also deeper thoughts. The disappearance of the Legassicks, and the tortuous beatings after their departure by Miss Silverwood, had left terrible, unhealed mental scars.

On Sunday at the church service, I watched as Uncle William climbed the pulpit stairs, and heard him preach the sermon entitled, 'Everyone is a Somebody to God'. His words were very meaningful but left me very distraught. I thought of the aftermath of their departure and the 'Nobody's Child in a Black Gymslip' reflection in the mirror in Rothwell. I wanted to share with them my feelings and memories, but withheld the details, fearing it would upset them. Auntie Agnes knew what had happened, but she did not betray my confidence.

Tearful farewells were said on the day of our flight home to Leeds. The pink elephant dress stayed in the wardrobe, never to be seen again. On the aeroplane, Auntie Agnes cuddled me. She said she had been worried I would not need her now I had found the Legassicks again. I hadn't realised the emotional impact the holiday had upon her. This was yet another occasion when I became aware of the great love she had for me, and how in all things she put my interests and well-being before her own.

Twenty One

BICYCLE RIDES

Shortly after our visit to Jersey, an old bicycle frame had come my way. New tyres were purchased and our neighbour kindly fitted brakes and a bell. The bicycle was stored in the cellar and had to be carried up and down the well-worn stone steps. I was a strong, healthy fourteen-year-old, so this was no burden to me.

I spent many happy hours cycling around Holbeck and beyond. I still owned a watch I had received from both aunts on my eleventh birthday and was able to return home at the given time. I had worked out how long it would take me to cycle into Leeds and to the address inside my father's gift.

Having sought permission to stay out longer, I took off in the direction of Leeds and soon found the address. I was sure I had been in this street before with Miss Goddard, my first social worker. Making enquiries in the community, I was informed that an old lady who shared my surname had lived in this street long ago. When she became frail and unable to care for herself, she had been transferred to South Lodge, the old workhouse for the Holbeck area of Leeds.

This complex was practically next door to my school and only a few streets away from where I was now living. The building was no longer a workhouse and it was under reconstruction for use as an old people's home. I knew the building and the grounds well, having passed them so many times, both on my way to church and school. I felt deeply saddened that I did not know my own paternal grandmother had been there.

One person was able to recollect that my grandmother had had four sons. Giving a lot of thought to these details, I realised that if my grandmother had four sons and one was my father, I must also have three uncles. Depending on their ages, I could possibly also have cousins. At last, I was beginning to feel like I belonged to someone. I also had surnames, as their surnames would all be the same. I felt certain the little old lady lying in bed who I had been taken to see as a very small child had been my paternal grandmother. Tears flowed as I cycled home, but I hid them, along with my newfound knowledge, from my two aunties.

★★★

Returning to school for the first time since the accident, I was told that the last afternoon lesson was to be domestic science. At lunchtime, I took home the list of ingredients required. Auntie Agnes went around to the local corner shop and purchased all I needed. It was quite expensive, and money was tight, but she would not have let me face the wrath of the teacher had I failed to prepare for the cookery lesson.

When I entered the classroom, the cookery teacher referred to me as 'the brat with the gammy leg'. At first, I was shocked at her remark, but laughed it off. I finished baking my cake and was standing by the door waiting to collect our baking at the end of the session. The teacher accused me of not informing the class the week before that they were to bring in tins for their cake. I told her that I had only just returned to school. Turning angrily towards me, she shouted, 'Do not cheek me, you illegitimate brat!'

I was horrified. I was no stranger to the word 'illegitimate', having heard it said so often in Rothwell. I knew its meaning. I had been reassured by both my aunts that I was not illegitimate: my father was well known and I was born in wedlock. I glared at this person who had dared to refer to me in such a vulgar manner. I stormed out of the classroom with my hands very firmly in my pockets. I was so angry I wanted to let her feel the power of my discus-throwing muscles! Instead, I cried. I waited until she had left the room and then returned to collect my sponge cake.

I found the teacher's references and humiliation very distressing. Several girls in my class tried to comfort me. One girl went to the headmistress and told her what she had just heard the teacher call me. I was inconsolable.

The duty social worker visited me. I told her about the teacher's remarks, adding that some of the girls' fathers had attended the school already. I was the only one whose father was not available to attend and stop this horrible woman in her tracks. Mr Purnell was the only person I knew who could have intervened, but he had hundreds of children in care so nothing was done.

Since returning from Jersey, the slightest provocation led to such tearful episodes. I could not reason with my feelings. I had gone from feeling so happy and contented with my home life to feeling distressed and fearful of school, the latter due only to the one domestic science teacher. I was also deeply troubled by my memories of the contrasts between the days when the Legassicks had made such a fuss of me, and the violent abuse I had suffered at the hands of Silverwood. So many memories had come flooding back.

I longed for peace from the inner turmoil. As a little child I shared my worries with Auntie Agnes, but as a teenager, I was inclined to bottle things up until the emotional bubble burst. I knew the people who really loved and cared for me were my two foster aunts, who only ever wanted the best in life for me.

At home, I had the most caring and comfortable environment any young person could crave. I was kept immaculately clean and tidy despite the minimal facilities available. Even though there was a small allowance sent for me each week, along with pocket money from the Social Work Department, I knew there were times when the old-age pensions were used to supplement any extras. I literally lacked nothing that was essential to my well-being. If something was needed for body and soul, it would be provided first; wants were second on the list and provided if sufficient funds were available. Material wants were only purchased after savings were put aside from my pocket money allowance. I was taught to avoid debt or hire purchase, as it was known in those days.

However, I could never purchase my particular wants with money – I wanted Kevin, and I wanted to know my identity. I wanted to be free from the authorities who restricted any normal family life to committee meetings and long-winded consents.

I lay awake at night, trying to work out the best way forward with my family search. I reasoned that, if I had been so near to one grandmother, could I have been as close to the other? I wondered if I had family connections in the village of Rothwell where I had spent my early years.

I planned to lend my bicycle to a friend at school. I would collect it after lunch and then abscond from school. This would give me a few hours' freedom to cycle to the place of such bad memories. I knew Miss Silverwood was no more, so I plucked up courage, deceived my dear foster aunts for the first time, and arrived in Rothwell safely.

Many things had changed, but I was soon talking to people who had lived there for years. I recognised two people who had attended the church, but they showed no recognition of me. After all, I had been one in a large crowd.

Calling at one house, I asked the owner if she knew anyone by the name of Mabel Ellis.

'Yes,' the woman replied, 'Mabel lives at the top of the road. Do you know where the old orphanage was? She lives in the next street.'

I could hardly believe what I was hearing. Within minutes, I was standing before Mabel. 'I think you might be related to me,' I said.

'I know who you are,' said my maternal grandmother.

'How do you know who I am?'

'Because you used to live over there,' she said, pointing to where the remains of the walls and black wrought-iron gates were now crumbling away.

How often I must have seen the roof and chimney pots of Granny's house as I rattled the swing chains. Had I passed her as I walked with the other orphans in crocodile form on Sundays or to school on weekdays? My thoughts raced around in my head. I could not hold back the tears; neither could my grandmother.

'Come in. I'll put the kettle on,' said Granny. I was home at last!

Our cups of tea were getting cold as we asked each other so many questions. My first question, 'Why did you not come to see me?', brought a most unexpected answer.

'Because the authorities said I was to keep away from you as you were up for adoption with a minister and his wife, and you were very happy!'

Granny's deep-blue eyes fixed my gaze. 'Are you happy', she asked?'

'I am, now I have found you,' I said, giving her my first hug.

Twenty Two

DEAR OLD GRANNY

Darkness was falling as I rounded the corner into Mario Street. My right knee was aching terribly, and the cobbled streets only emphasised how saddle sore I felt. Opening the door, ready to sincerely apologise for my late return, I was greeted by Miss Foster. Auntie Agnes was sitting by the fireside in tears, believing I may have suffered some misadventure. I went over to her and hugged her close to me. I was so ashamed of my own thoughtlessness and the obvious pain I had caused her.

'Where have you been?' she asked.

'I have found my real grandmother,' I replied.

Miss Foster asked which grandmother. I replied that I knew about both of them but had only visited the maternal one.

'You are not supposed to be visiting your family without the committee's permission,' she said, in a rather panicky voice.

Before she could say another word, I made it very clear to her that she would not stop me seeing any of my relatives. I told her how disgusted I was to have been both deceived and denied my rights of knowledge or access to my grandmother, who had told me of her deepest desire to keep in touch with me. I related how my grandmother had said she had watched me day after day through the wrought-iron gates in front of Rothwell Children's Home. Eventually, she had heard I was to be adopted by a minister and his wife.

I wanted to know why she had not been told that I had never been adopted by anyone.

Miss Foster sat silently staring into the fire. Auntie Agnes crossed the room and took me lovingly in her arms. Tears trickled down her cheeks. 'I want you to know I will always love you,' she said. I sensed her fear of losing me. I loved her deeply, but I longed to know my true identity.

'By the way, I am going back to see my granny tomorrow,' I said.

Miss Foster got up from her seat. Putting on her coat, she told Auntie Agnes she would come back on Monday. I was to be kept home from school.

'Who cares? It's cookery class,' I said belligerently.

After my social worker had made her hasty retreat, I asked Auntie Agnes why she had visited yet again. She had been coming to the house so much since our return from Jersey. As she always sent me away to the bedroom and spoke to my aunt alone, I had no idea what the reason was for this new pattern of contact. I felt it was overpowering and distressing me.

As Auntie Agnes and I sat by the roaring fire, I related to her all the day's events. I was reprimanded for taking time off school without her knowledge. The dangers of my journey were also highlighted.

I apologised and promised I would not do that again. I was humbled by her account of her fears for my safety, and all the anxious thoughts she had since what would have been home time. I heard how she had visited the school, only to find it was closed and the staff all away home. Due to my absence, she had no choice but to notify Social Services.

She asked what my grandmother was like. I described this lovely old lady, perched on a high wooden stool near a fireplace, so similar to the one we were both sitting beside at present. I described Granny's beautiful blue eyes, moistened with tears and her snowy white hair glistening in the firelight. I looked into the face of this dear elderly lady, now sitting beside me and I knew she had also wept tears for me so many times over many years.

I shared with Auntie Agnes how I had promised to return the next day and I didn't want to break that promise. Auntie Agnes understood my desire to keep my promise; after all, she had been the person who always taught me 'never to make a promise, unless you can keep it'. I was going to meet my uncle, Granny's son, who shared the house in Rothwell with her.

Assuring me she would not stand in my way now that I had found my own family and Miss Foster was aware, my dear aunt conceded to the visit on the strictest promise that I went by bus to Rothwell and returned home at the appointed time. I asked if she wanted to come with me, but she felt this would not be wise – she was still under tight obligation not to relate confidential matters regarding my history. From this remark, I realised even Auntie Agnes had had to withhold vital information from me. I didn't, in any way, blame her. I was all too aware of the closed-file system and hated it. Now I held some power at last.

I may have held the power, but I was soon to learn that I lacked wisdom.

The next day, Auntie Agnes travelled to Leeds with me. We stopped at the market and bought flowers for Granny. I was accompanied to the Rothwell bus stance and given clear instructions and sufficient money for my return journey. My temper of the previous night had cooled, and now as Auntie Agnes and I parted, we both cried. I had such torn loyalties. I genuinely did not want to hurt my two foster aunts, but I desperately wanted to be part of my own real family.

At Granny's house, the kettle was boiling merrily on the fire range. The table was laid with a clean, but well-worn tablecloth. Granny arranged her flowers in a jam jar and put them proudly in the centre of the table.

Coffee was served in half-pint pots and the homemade Yorkshire parkin biscuits were delicious. I was offered a second biscuit, but something within me made me realise Granny was very poor, so I declined.

My uncle arrived back from the fish shop. He placed the newspaper-wrapped fish and chips in the fire oven to keep warm. He turned and, taking me in his arms, hugged me and welcomed me back into my real family.

I asked where Kevin was and was very disappointed when neither my granny nor uncle could tell me anything about his whereabouts. They too had hoped I would have the answer to this burning question. Sadly, I heard that my mother's whereabouts were unknown. Apparently, she was Granny's eldest daughter and one of five children. All I could learn was that she had gone away, years ago, with a travelling man. I realised then how much her mother and brother longed to see her.

We all sat round the fire and enjoyed our first meal together. The wrappings were carefully folded and laid aside for the next day's firelighter. We talked well into the afternoon, but my eye was constantly observing the time on my watch, which differed from the time on Granny's clock. As my watch was synchronised with the clock on the mantel piece at Mario Street, I chose to use it to adhere to my promised return timetable. When I asked if I could use the toilet, Granny apologetically told me it was two doors away down the street. I laughed and taking the key for the midden, I boasted mine was three doors away down the street!

I travelled back to Mario Street and arrived on schedule. Here, the tea table was laid with its usual lace-edged white cloth and the delicate china dishes. Auntie Cissie had returned from a holiday after visiting her friend in East Kilbride, Scotland, and she was busy toasting some bread by the fireside. I knew by her reaction that she was obviously saddened by events at school, but she stated that she fully understood my need to trace my own family.

I recounted the details of my visit to Rothwell. I realised there was a sense of relief, tinged with sadness, in the home. My aunts no longer had to keep vital family details from me. This was a burden they must have carried, especially in the early years of our friendship, as I had an inquisitive mind and was not easily placated with simple answers.

Auntie Cissie had a real capacity for sensing distress in people and an incredible way of gentle counselling that allowed expression of feelings. I shared with her how I couldn't understand why I had been denied contact with my maternal grandmother when she had shown genuine interest in me and lived so close to me. How comforting it would have been for me to know I did belong to somebody. I was wanted by my grandmother. I reasoned, if Miss Silverwood had known that I had a relative living close by, she may have been less likely to inflict such brutality upon me.

There had been no legal intervention or court order preventing my grandmother's contact. The only explanation had been that the committee had said no to any contact. I told my foster aunts that I felt so upset and angry that I wanted to punch the committee's lights out for the awful way they had treated my real family. Auntie Cissie gave me a very disapproving glance.

I was so frustrated that I had never been allowed to say to the committee members how I felt, even when I was old enough to make some informed choices. In the meantime, my grandmother had lived with guilt feelings that I was in Rothwell Children's Home, a place where the locals knew that some children suffered brutality by certain members of staff. I felt distressed and utterly confused, having been so deceived by the authorities and for so long.

'Let us say a prayer and ask God's blessing upon all your family,' said Auntie Cissie. We bowed our heads in prayer and I knew I was truly forgiven. I also knew my foster aunts understood my heart's desire.

During the following weeks, my sleep pattern was so disturbed. I attempted to pray about the circumstances surrounding my family, but strangely enough, I found prayer times were also a struggle. I could not reason with the distressing thoughts regarding the recent discovery of my own grandmother, her sense of loss, and her attempts to maintain contact with me after she discovered I was in care.

I look back on this day with mixed emotions: if only wisdom could sit on young shoulders, I would have made fewer mistakes! (I was later to learn that Miss Foster was facing her own family crisis and caring for her sick mother. Auntie Agnes had been a support and confidante to her during these stressful times – hence the extra visits to Mario Street.)

Twenty Three

PROLONGED SCHOOL DAYS

On Sunday morning, the walk to church with Auntie Agnes was far from the usual pleasant time, due to no fault of ours. Passing South Lodge, the old workhouse for the Holbeck area of Leeds, it now seemed dark and forbidding. I was distressed to think that my paternal grandmother had been there, possibly during the time that it had been used as an old people's refuge. I recall how the older generation in the community spoke of the workhouse with real dread, as a grim place to be avoided at all costs. I had for many years passed by on the other side, unaware of my grandmother's existence.

I, too, had known what it was like for others to cross the road and pass by as though I, along with the other children in care, were untouchable rejects of society without ever having committed a crime. During the afternoon Salvation Army meeting, I sat and cried. Comforted by Auntie Cissie, I left before the service ended. Friends at both places of worship showed me such kindness but my mind was in utter turmoil.

I awoke early on Monday morning and, dressed in my school uniform, awaited Miss Foster's arrival. Together we walked in absolute silence to school. I was left sitting outside the headmistress's office for more than an hour before being summoned into her presence.

I was amazed at her gentle approach towards me. There was no anger or caning. (I had never seen or heard of any caning in this school, but somehow thought my absconding might warrant it.) I was informed by Miss Beresford that as I had been off school so long with the knee injury, it had been decided I would be allowed to stay on longer at school until I was sixteen.

I was horrified! After all, we were only weeks away from school-leaving day. Even the last school dance had been arranged and my new dancing outfit had been especially bought for the occasion, including my first pair of nylon stockings! I protested against such action. I wanted to leave school at fifteen like all my classmates. I quickly visualised how this could be seen as favouritism or, worse, punishment!

Turning directly to me, Miss Foster spelled out my fate. The committee and Educational Board had met several weeks ago and decided this was the best option for me. So, this had nothing to do with my recent escapades! There had been no indication of any of these plans relayed to me and I had never been asked for my opinion. How I detested this confounded committee gathering and its insensitivity to my feelings. Surely, at fifteen and about to enter the world of work, I at least had the right (if not the brains) to be included in the decision-making process? I was not just an agenda number: I was a young person with real feelings, hopes and aspirations. More than a few doors were slammed in school that day.

Mrs Fletcher and Mrs Sanderson both indicated that I would no longer be in their classes, and I was so sad when I heard this. Both teachers had been kind to me, and through their efforts I had started to improve in many subjects. Discovering I had no option but to accept the terms as set down in my absence, I reasoned I would do my best, at least for my foster aunts, the two teachers and headmistress, whom I greatly respected.

When I heard I would be transferred to Miss Sheridan's class, I was terrified. This was the last news I wanted to hear. I certainly knew of this teacher's formidable, disciplinarian reputation. I also knew of her church connections – she served on many church committees. I was aware of her contacts with the Legassicks and knew that she maintained regular contact with them. Two things were in her favour: her wonderful singing voice, so often heard in the church choir and school assemblies, and her brilliant mathematical brain. I knew my maths would never stand up to her scrutiny!

★★★

A few weeks later, the razzmatazz of the school-leaving dance was well under way. Our school had been the chosen venue. The hall had been decorated with streamers and balloons, some with the names of the school leavers written on them. Mine, of course, was not there.

Dressed in my new finery, I was desperately trying to forget the discomfort of wearing the new, white, lacy suspender belt I had purchased with my pocket money allowance. The button that was intended to stay in its metal loop was too small and kept coming out of its socket, releasing a pleated nylon down my leg in a most irritating way, resulting in several giggling trips to the cloakroom. A friend lent me a silver sixpence to use as a makeshift button and showed me how to wrap the stocking top around it before poking it though the suspender loop.

I wore my first short skirt (minis were the latest fashion) with some pride. I even forgot about the long scar on my right leg. There was a real air of excitement in the girls' cloakroom, and a great flurry of activity as girls powdered noses and dabbed Coty L'Aimant or Evening in Paris perfume behind ears. A friend's bright red lipstick would not have pleased my Salvationist friends, who reasoned that the price of it would buy a poor old soul a cup of tea or necessary food, but I wore it with pride along with the borrowed rouge and face powder.

Groups of handsome boys, gathered from local segregated schools, were sheepishly sitting at the back of the hall. A few of my schoolfriends' younger brothers were also there.

I saw Brian, a boy who had once lived only four doors away down Mario Street. He, along with his family, had since transferred to Middleton, one of the newly constructed council estates around Leeds where former slum dwellers were being rehoused under the Leeds City Renovation Schemes. Recognising me, he came over and asked me to dance.

We danced together for the whole evening to rock-and-roll music, and country and western songs, which ended for me with a sore knee. I was so proud to have been chosen by Brian as his dance partner and elated when he asked me if he could walk me home. In my ecstasy, I had forgotten to wash my face of its colourful hues and received an inquisitive look from my two aunts. They thanked Brian for bringing me home safely.

A few days later, I was invited to Middleton. I was amazed at the size of the new estate with its three-bedroomed houses and large gardens. How I hoped that, when the time came for Mario Street to meet the power of the bulldozer, we too would have a house near Brian's.

The last day of term arrived. During the school assembly, Miss Beresford wished all the leavers three things: good health, good friends and long lives of happiness. She told all those gathered that money would not bring them these things. To work hard and earn enough for your keep and a little put away for a rainy day was recommended. I had so often heard this last statement at home and its philosophy was sound. Tearful goodbyes were said as our class parted at the school gates. I felt so isolated and alone when the girls I had known and grown to like so much went their separate ways.

★★★

Throughout the school holidays I cycled to Rothwell many times, with full permission from Auntie Agnes and timely returns from me. I had discovered by chance that, now I had found members of my family, there was little the authorities could do to prevent me seeing them, as long as there were no detrimental circumstances where the law could step in.

My grandmother was certainly a woman of good character. Several of her neighbours testified to her accounts of regular visits to the orphanage gates. She had always shown an interest in me, which had been thwarted by the authorities. Her home was very poorly furnished, but spotlessly clean. My uncle would say his mother made him scrub the floor until sparks came off the brush!

I heard the sad story of how my grandfather and a work colleague had been in a brawl and they were unable to pay the imposed fines. For reasons unknown, even to Granny, both men were locked up in Stanley Royd, the local mental asylum, where my grandfather died, leaving Granny to raise five children alone. Granny always maintained that my grandfather was beaten and severely injured by a warden, as she had seen for herself his heavily bruised body only days before his death.

Life thereafter was extremely hard, but Granny was a proud woman and managed to take in washing and do other menial tasks in order to support her family. When her own health failed, and before the introduction of the 1948 Welfare State, she had to rely on Parish financial support to help feed and support the children. I was taken to see other aunts and uncles and a large number of cousins, both male and female. I soon realised I was from a large family on the maternal side. (Little was known about my father's family's whereabouts. A few last sightings were given, but they went back many years.)

As a young man, my uncle had got in with the wrong crowd and fallen foul of the law, for which he received a short prison sentence, shortened further by his good behaviour. This information was all the committee members had needed to try to block my visits. My uncle had since turned his life around for the better and he held down a good job with a local firm. He certainly treated me with respect and kindness, and I liked him as a person and was unafraid in his company.

I was called into headquarters on several occasions. More than one social worker tried to put over to me that it was undesirable for me to be visiting Rothwell. However, to say that blood was thicker than water was an understatement. I vigorously defended my newfound family members.

My uncle had explained his circumstances in full to me on my second visit to his mother's home and the office staff failed to understand that I had attended the Salvation Army for years and knew of the change in the lives of some former wrongdoers. I also lived with two remarkable Christian ladies who spent hours supporting society failures and who had brought many to new and better ways. What right had anyone to condemn someone who had turned his life around for the good?

Unfortunately, one day my uncle made an off-the-cuff statement publicly, saying that if we were not related he would have married me. Someone rang Social Services.

I had another visit from Miss Foster and a barrage of questions followed. I was asked if I knew what sex was. I answered, 'Do you think I have come out of a conjurer's hat? Of course, I do. Six comes after five.' There was a peal of laughter from the room and a few hands covered mouths. It dawned on me that I thought she had said 'six' not 'sex'. Perhaps I had come out of a conjurer's hat after all!

Within days of this incident, a letter arrived from Miss Foster instructing Auntie Agnes to take me for a routine medical. I was taken to the doctors and put through numerous tests. Auntie Agnes was instructed that the tablets I was prescribed were to be given me for two weeks, then two weeks without. This routine was to be repeated. I was told the pills were for my spotty teenage face.

Within days of taking the tablets I felt so ill. I had severe headaches, a bloated feeling in my stomach and severe cramp-like feelings in my lower abdomen, and my concentration levels were very poor. The doctor was called and insisted that I persevere with the medication as the symptoms would subside. Unfortunately, they only subsided on the days when I didn't have to take them. My spotty face was much more desirable than any pills, especially as the spots were only supposed to last through my teenage years. The way I was feeling I would have gladly ditched the tablets and remained spotty.

★★★

I met up with some of my former school friends and heard how successful most had been in acquiring work. Some were receiving reasonable pay packets and treated themselves to new clothes. They looked so grown up in their chosen outfits and fancy hairstyles.

I was certainly not excluded from any of their social activities. Invitations were given and the friends waited patiently for my authorisation letters. Even my friends now knew the authoritarian system I lived under.

I never saw Brian again. I heard he, too, had a good job. I don't suppose he would want to keep going out with a schoolgirl!

★★★

I had outgrown my school blazer and finances were tight. Auntie Agnes bought a small length of navy barathea (a material used in the manufacture of quality coats and blazers) and using all her sewing skills, she carefully unpicked my old blazer, turned the material and added inserts where needed to extend its size. It was so professionally done that it appeared to be brand new. I was extremely grateful for her expertise and her desire to send me back to school suitably dressed.

Very reluctantly, I returned to the school and took my place amongst the fourteen-year olds. Miss Sheridan lived up to her reputation. In the second lesson, maths, she called me out to the blackboard to do an equation. I had missed lessons on equations given by Mrs Sanderson due to the accident and subsequent absence from school. I told Miss Sheridan I hadn't done this form of maths.

'Sit down, you stupid girl, and let a fourteen-year-old show you how it's done!' she bellowed.

I did not sit down. I lifted my school bag, walked out of the class and straight to Miss Beresford's office. Now in floods of tears, I told her I wanted my report book – I was leaving school.

'I cannot let you leave school as you do not have a birth certificate, and therefore cannot be issued with a National Insurance Number allowing you to seek work,' said the headmistress.

I couldn't believe what I was hearing. Surely there was some mistake? After all, I had been in care since the age of three – plenty of time for the authorities to acquire some identity for me. So this was the true reason why I had to stay at school for another term!

I was absolutely shocked. I was adamant that I would leave school and somehow make my own way. After much coaxing, Miss Beresford relented and went to get my report book, saying she would have to contact Social Services. As she tried to unlock the cupboard, the key stuck. I said I would try release it with my penknife. Taking the tiny pearl-handled knife I had carried for years to sharpen my pencil (most children had something similar), I proceeded to move the locking device across, releasing the door.

At that moment, Miss Sheridan entered the room. Hastily, she turned and fled up the corridor, shouting to the secretary to telephone the police. Miss Beresford, realising what had happened, called out to her, but the deed was done.

The police arrived, and I left with them to go to the station. A statement was taken, and Miss Beresford clearly stated I had never threatened her. (I still hold evidence of this correspondence to this day.) Surprisingly, my little knife was handed back to me.

I treasured this little pocket knife. It had been given to me for use at school and in the children's home's garden for cutting the string used to tie up plants. I had also used it many times during holidays at Leighton Buzzard. It had been given to me by a kind old friend.

That day's episode was to set me on a collision course I never could have dreamt would occur. I was taken back to Auntie Agnes, who was deeply distressed by the circumstances. Miss Foster arrived with a male social worker who I had often seen around headquarters.

This big portly man started to throw his weight around verbally the moment he stepped in the door. Both my aunts tried to reason with him to hear my version of events first, but to no avail. But I was now ready for him. I had had enough of the stifling effects of Social Services. To me, I was again a 'Nobody': I didn't even have a birth certificate!

I reasoned that if I had been treated the same as other school leavers, I would not be in this position. I felt the committee's intentions had not been honourable; they were covering up a huge mistake at my expense. Their lack of understanding of my feelings now deserved my defensive verbal onslaught. I berated them for their underhand ways.

Auntie Agnes assured me she had only discovered this error a few weeks previously and had tried to acquire a certificate for me, but as she was not related, she was officially unable to get a copy of my original certificate. However, an abbreviated certificate had been ordered. The male social worker raised the matter of my family visits. I told him I would not stop until I had found Kevin and asked what right they had to separate us as little children.

'You will not find Kevin!' blurted out this man, standing with his face inches away from mine. I asked where Kevin was now. Without any hesitation, the answer returned, 'Legally adopted. Don't you remember the last time you saw him when he was four? That was the same day he went to his new family.' I was horrified at his blatant ignorance and gross insensitivity.

In my fifteen years, I had coped with so many abusive or difficult situations with tantrums, tears or total withdrawal into a sullen world. Now I raged. I yelled and screamed at this man who had such audacity to spell this out to me so crudely and boastfully. My dear aunties, sensing my utter distress, came across to comfort me. I pushed them both away. A neighbour, who had been so kind to me over the years, heard the shouting and came to the door; she, too, was pushed away. I told her to leave me alone.

The social worker shouted as much as I did. He had also lost the plot.

Finally, words failed. I sat on the edge of the stone sink and the floodgates opened. All attempts to comfort me were rebuffed. I was inconsolable. I felt my world had emptied of all its meaning. It seemed I would never again see my brother, Kevin. I reached out to the gas cooker and turned the taps on. Dear Auntie Agnes came and turned them off. She took me into her arms and said, 'Please don't, we love you.'Tears streamed down her cheeks and seeing this made me cry even more.

At this point, the male social worker must have realised his folly. He softened and tried to comfort me. He said he was deeply sorry but he thought I knew about Kevin's adoption. I asked if Kevin's other name was Michael.

'Yes. His name is Kevin Michael; he has gone to a good Christian family and is doing well.'

I turned to Auntie Agnes and asked her if she knew about Kevin.

In her honest way, she answered, 'Yes. I was under strict obligation not to tell you.'

I looked at Auntie Cissie. She nodded her head, confirming that she also knew the circumstances. I felt absolutely devastated. Why had I never been given such vital information?

Miss Foster had left the house. Within a short time, a car drew up at the door and I was taken to Street Lane Reception Centre. I was soon standing in the same hall where Kevin and I had been separated so many years before, and where I had last seen my father.

The isolation room was to be my bedroom. I did not need to be shown the way around the home – I already knew it all too well. Nothing had changed.

A few hours later, everything I owned at Auntie Agnes's home was delivered by the duty social worker to my room. I was told in a brusque manner that I was not to visit Mario Street again.

***

I was unfamiliar with the medical term 'depression', but I knew such deep sorrow and heartache. In that moment, I felt nothing but a deep sense of despair and foreboding. I had always kept my mind focussed on one day tracing Kevin. I had come so near to finding my real parents, but at great emotional cost.

During the past few months, I had coped with the accident at school, followed by the emotional reunion with Auntie Marjorie and Uncle

William after nine years' separation. I was also coping with the terrible mood swings that had started when the medication for my so-called spots had been prescribed.

I had discovered so many facts relating to my admission into the homes and, more recently, I had been literally forced against my will to stay on at school due to an error at headquarters. Now I had been so insensitively informed that my brother Kevin and I had been legally separated via the adoption process.

This last episode left me feeling utterly confused. If it was true that Kevin had been legally adopted, any reunion, if that were still possible, could have huge emotional impact on Kevin's present life. This would also be such an emotional situation for his adoptive parents, whom I reasoned must have loved him enough to adopt him in the first place. That day, I mentally closed the door on the world.

Kevin, aged four, on the steps of Rachael Nursery, Street Lane, Leeds. The day he ate my chocolate bar!

Twenty Four

SIBLINGS HAVE RIGHTS

A faint knock on the bedroom door disturbed my thoughts. The handle turned, and a little face peered round. Standing there in a pink floral dress was a little girl of about six years. Her blonde, tousled curls partly fell over her deep blue eyes. 'Hello. I've come to show you where the dining room is,' she said in her childish voice.

I blinked back the tears. I knew where the dining room was; hadn't I had many meals beneath its roof? The child took hold of my hand and told me to hurry up and follow her. Obediently, I followed. Entering the dining room was like stepping back in time. The segregated staff table was covered with a white table cloth and laden with grapefruit, cereals and toast, followed by cooked breakfast, all served by a resident. The children's tables were bare wood, scrubbed almost white, where the food consisted of porridge, bread and butter. The last time I saw such practices was in Rothwell, many years ago and I couldn't believe that these Dickensian ways could still exist.

I thought back to Miss Smith's home and her family-orientated care, where we were all were treated as equals. I also knew from Miss Smith's teaching on budgeting that there was an allotted food allowance for each resident with exactly the same allowance for staff. Here, the children were being denied the good wholesome food provided by Social Services. All the homes had a weekly delivery of food and other supplies that came from the same warehouse in Leeds. Why, I questioned, were the children deprived of the same standard of meals eaten by the staff?

After breakfast, the same little child invited me to play with her. She was not going to school that day as she was having visitors. The playroom was still at the end of the corridor, as it had been in my early days. On the way, I noticed that hygiene standards were poor and there was a smell of dampness about the place.

Having spent some time in this little girl's presence, I began to slowly unwind and relax. She wanted me to dress up as a princess. Her innocent play, with the fake tiara that she insisted I put on my head and silver shoes that barely covered my toes, helped me to laugh again. I reasoned it would not be long before a penny peep show (our name for the selection process) would be staged, and this little child would disappear to a new foster home or 'who knows where'. I wished her love, stability and happiness.

I heard a group of people gathering in the staff room, and the smell of coffee drifted by. I was called to the office. Sitting there in tears was Miss Sheridan. Having realised her mistake regarding the penknife incident and all that followed, she had been unable to sleep and was desperate to see me. I was so unsure of my feelings towards her. I hated to see others cry, so I crossed the room and stretched out my hand towards hers. She grasped mine and said how sorry she was. I believed her. When she said that yesterday had been a terrible day, I wholeheartedly agreed with her.

Her formidable character was now far from evident. I felt this was a real act of sincerity. I apologised for leaving her class in haste. We were left alone and talked through the present situation. My self-esteem was so low I could hardly reason with her constant advice to come back to school. I told her I was no longer allowed to live at Auntie Agnes's home. She was obviously shocked at this news, which had not been conveyed to her.

I realised that her bark was worse than her bite. Beneath the hard exterior was a person with compassion and, above all, honesty. She assured me that if there was anything she could do to help me I was to call her number, which she wrote on a piece of paper and gave to me. We parted at the front door. If only I could turn back the clock and get to know her – perhaps I could actually learn equations!

A few days later, Uncle William was standing at the same office door. He was over from Jersey to attend a ministerial conference. He advised me that he had heard of the recent events and how depressed I was. He asked numerous questions about my real family, and I sensed someone had talked things over with him. I refrained from giving any information regarding these matters. When I asked if he knew that Kevin was legally adopted, he agreed he did know. Seemingly, Kevin had been adopted about the same time as I had met Uncle William and Auntie Marjorie. It seemed I was the only person denied the knowledge of Kevin's adoption for all those years. Now I wanted to be left alone. After all, who could I trust?

How much easier it would have been if I had been told as a little child that Kevin had a new home, so I could have become accustomed to the facts and, above all, had all these caring people to support me, instead of the terrible mistrust I now harboured, and against my better judgement. If only we had been given our family human rights to stay together as siblings, I would not have suffered the shock I now felt. I wondered how many more young children would face the same situation. I had known so many who talked of missing brothers and sisters. They, too, had been denied the company of their siblings.

★★★

I began to settle back into the daily institutional life. With time alone and a morning routine of ironing mountains of communal clothing, I reflected on the situation I now faced. When I asked permission to go to Rothwell, my request was refused. I tried another tactic. I asked why I had not been given my pocket money allowance (all children in care have this weekly allowance). A rather red-faced matron produced a jar of half-crowns from the medicine cabinet and gave me one. I soon told her that I was due seven shillings and six pence, three half-crowns, having now spent three weeks under her so-called care. Equations I may not have known, but I could count my money, and reluctantly she handed over the coins.

Permission was granted for me to go for a walk each afternoon. I behaved impeccably for the first few outings and returned on time. Having purchased some writing paper and stamps, I sent off letters to all and sundry, including my real family. A letter to my foster aunts remained unanswered.

I was devastated. No post was returned – something was wrong. I knew they, at least, would reply. In my letter to my real uncle, I mentioned my daily walk. Within days, we were meeting at the weekends as his work prevented daily visits.

Other members of the family sometimes came along and I was told how they had visited the headquarters for permission to take me out. It had been denied. Our secret meetings continued until the matron's husband, Mr Gallantry, saw me walking through Roundhay Park with my uncle and two cousins.

Now, for the first time, I was to experience 'pin down'. This practice of removing the child's clothing and locking them in a room for hours was a practice not unknown by some social workers at the time. Mr Gallantry failed to remember that my suitcase full of clothes from Mario Street was lying under the bed. Redressing, I was able to leave the room through the window as the isolation room was on ground level. I soon cleared a pathway through the rose bed.

I found an old bicycle in a shed at the rear of the building and cycled to Roundhay Park and returned through Shadwell, a lovely conservation village situated at the far end of park, and back along the main road to the reception centre. I re-entered the building a few hours later via the same window. Surprisingly, I was not missed on this occasion.

My plan was to take clothing and hide it somewhere to be collected later, should pin down become a regular feature. It certainly did.

Every afternoon, instead of being allowed out, I was subjected to this practice for a week. The weather was atrocious, so I chose to stay in the warmth and re-read some of the books from my suitcase. I was gradually coming under the control of the system through lack of human contact with the outside world.

My Unseen Guest was all I clung to in those dark days. Each night, I curled up in my special foetal position of early childhood, but now I prayed and cried before sleep brought another day. I prayed for the strength to get through each day. I also prayed for forgiveness for the way I had handled recent events. I thought of the words I had so often heard both my foster aunts say: 'Nothing is impossible for God to change, but He doesn't force himself upon you. Ask, believing, and He will help you.'

Eventually, I planned to run away for good.

I left, one evening, by my bedroom window. I was so naïve that I failed to take enough warm clothing, and soon felt so cold and hungry. I kept walking until I was stopped by a lorry driver and offered a lift. He asked where I was heading.

'Scarcroft,' I said, only knowing the name of the place through church outings. This same driver put me down in the village – I look back with real gratitude for his decency. The night was wet and very cold.

I am unsure why I telephoned Mr Gallantry to say I was there, but fear of being alone could have been a factor. A kindly policewoman returned me to Street Lane Reception Centre. After leaving me there alone, I soon felt the fists of a most violent Mr Gallantry. I took the blows with my own fists tightly clenched and in my pockets. I would not break my vow not to retaliate.

But I was broken mentally. I tried to get out of the front door, but I was dragged back inside. I felt utterly exhausted and so afraid of this huge man with his thick moustache and deep, piercing eyes.

The bruises and 'pin down' contributed to my next action. The following day, I left via the window with only one desire: I wanted to die. I couldn't see my way out of this darkness and deep loneliness. I felt utterly deserted by everyone. I had no reason to live. I was being strenuously denied the right to family contact, and I had, through my actions, closed the door on all contact with my foster aunts and life beyond the homes. I had no hope of finding Kevin now he had been legally adopted.

The local chemist was only a few streets away. The aspirins were bought with my pocket money allowance and taken with copious amounts of water. The staff member who found me being sick called the ambulance.

St James Hospital in Leeds became my new address. After my initial recovery, I was allowed a visit from my uncle, who told me he had been very distressed by my reports of abuse in the Reception Centre. He had made regular visits to the area in the evenings, hoping to see me. On the night of my admission to hospital, he had hidden in the bushes and seen me carried out to the ambulance.

At the hospital, I told the medical staff what had happened to me, and how events had caused such a downturn in my life. The doctor I spoke to was very compassionate. He made it clear that I had rights and, in his opinion, those rights were being breached. He promised he would raise the issue with Social Services. Within hours, I was given full permission to contact my real family, but only the authorities could give consent for any foster family contact. (Of course, I am aware of the understandable rights of foster families to be consulted before renewing contact with foster children.)

Now, my uncle and grandmother were free, along with any other family and friends, to visit me with the doctor's full consent. I had at last left the children's homes, this time never to return.

However, I may have left the buildings but not the committee. The chairman was the first to visit. He genuinely appeared distressed by all the events that had taken place in his absence. I heard how he had been away from the office on a course. He was told about the bruises on my body on my admission to the hospital and appeared genuinely concerned about the 'pin down' reports. My only questions now related to Kevin. I wanted the truth of all the circumstances surrounding our separation. I was given as many details as legislation allowed.

★★★

Kevin's adoption was legalised when he was four. He was the little boy who had eaten the chocolate and had come back to me for more. His name was Kevin Michael. I was told he was adopted by a family living in Buckinghamshire. I listened intently.

A member of the Dean family lived in Aylesbury, Buckinghamshire. I had been to his home regularly on my Leighton Buzzard holidays. The two areas were so close and I knew both well. I wondered if I had ever passed Kevin on the street or in the town. This could have been a real possibility.

I asked if Kevin was happy and was told this was not known. Once the adoption had been finalised, the committee had no more jurisdiction unless a new referral was lodged. I asked if I could always keep a letter with any future address of mine in my family file in case Kevin ever wanted to find me. This action was agreed and I wrote the first of many letters, each giving details of my whereabouts.

However, the family search was not over. I still had the details to research of a foster parent's name that I had seen on my file. My family could shed no light on this, except to say that a taxi company in Swillington was called by the same name.

In the quietness of my side room at the hospital, I searched many telephone directories and found, to my surprise, an entry with the exact name and initials. Using the hospital phone, I was soon chatting away, not to Kevin, but to a hitherto unknown brother. Within days, just as I was leaving the ward for my daily exercise, I walked into the arms of my eldest stepbrother, Stanley. I discovered he was the son of my mother's first partner – my father had married my mother while she was pregnant and took on the responsibility for Stanley. With the family break-up, this same brother had also been taken into care and then fostered out.

The reunion was a wonderful occasion and hit the headlines: 'Girl Finds Brother She Never Knew Existed' blazed across the local Yorkshire papers and then went national.

★★★

'You are not allowed to visit your relatives.'

'Why not?' I asked, belligerently.

'Because I said so,' said the green-frocked nurse.

'Doctor Brown has given me full permission to visit all my relatives.'

'Doctor Brown is on holiday. Come with me!'

The nurse turned and strode hastily up the long hospital corridor. Without any hesitation or doubt to her motives, I follow obediently a few paces behind her. Ahead of us I could see another green-clad nurse standing by an open door. As we approached her, the first nurse spun round and pushed me through the open door, causing me to land heavily onto the floor. The door slammed shut. The key turned. I was imprisoned, unable to get out. The sound of their footsteps drifted away.

I was stunned with disbelief. I sat there for a few moments in absolute shock, overwhelmed with fear and panic. I stood up and went to the door, only to find it was without a door handle, and it was covered with a dark green, foam material. I touched the walls and found they were covered in a spongy coating. The same textured foam cladding covered every inch of the floor. The ceiling too had the same appearance as the walls. In the centre of the ceiling a heavy-looking wire guard covered the small lightbulb, casting an eerie, streaky pattern around the walls. So, this was a padded cell, a name I had heard from other patients, but had never seen before. Why, I reasoned, was I incarcerated here? Only the day before, nurses had gathered round me, whilst the local newspaper's photographer had taken our photographs, as I celebrated the first meeting with a newly traced brother.

The sound of approaching footsteps gave me some hope. The door opened and in rushed about six nurses. I was pinned to the floor and one nurse pulled down my clothing and thrust a sharp needle into my bottom. A bitter, sickly smell immediately came on my breath.

'Paraldehyde stinks!' said one nurse.

I vaguely remember an ambulance man saying to me, 'Be good, lass, and you will soon be released,' as he gently lifted me off a trolley and into a waiting bed. The days blurred in a foggy haze. Again, I was injected with the stinking drug and drifted off into what I hoped was a bad dream.

★★★

The action of the Children's Committee was swift and decisive. I was transferred to an old Victorian mental institution called Menston, later renamed Highroads' Hospital. Along with my Mario Street suitcases was a huge pile of letters and get-well cards addressed to me during my stay at Street Lane, which had been withheld from my sight. I was relieved to know that I had not been forgotten, but I was angry when I realised this was so reminiscent of my father's book, which I had also been denied.

I was locked into a ward with forty other patients with a wide variety of mental illnesses. I soon discovered that *some* were genuinely mentally ill. Others were women with babies that had been born out of wedlock years ago, which had led to their admission into this huge institution from where they had never been released, and there were people who had been returned to this country from war prisons as broken individuals. I heard some harrowing stories.

Being institutionalised did not impact on me too greatly; after all, I was a seasoned traveller to institutions. Being locked in, however, was very different. I was given a side room and told this was for my own protection. There were many night-time wanderers and this meant I was doubly locked in at night. Had a fire broken out, none of the patients in the side rooms would have survived! There was no escape once the doors were locked.

One night, the young woman in the next room to mine hanged herself. I was terrified when I heard the staff desperately trying to resuscitate her to no avail. For weeks I found it hard to sleep at night.

I witnessed the sadness and low morale of all the staff and patients in the ward. I vowed then that I would never again let suicidal thoughts take over my life. I was only sixteen years old and had hopes of better things to come.

A doctor saw me and said I was to be taken off the birth-control drugs. I was shocked. The tablets I had been given for a spotty face had, in fact, been a new oral birth-control medication. I wasn't even sexually active! I literally didn't know what sex was; this was a taboo subject. I am sure my maiden foster aunts would have found it hard to explain to me how babies were conceived.

Within weeks, I was beginning to feel more energetic. On the ward, a small financial allowance was given to me for helping with the bed-making duties. I graduated from this to helping to feed frail patients. The ward staff were tremendously kind to me, their youngest patient. I was taught how to dress the frail elderly, helped to bathe them and spent time taking them around the flowerbeds in the enclosed garden space.

On one occasion, I sat beside an old lady who was dying. The ward sister came and asked me if I wanted to leave the ward for a few hours. I had helped feed this lady many times and had grown to love her. I chose to stay and witnessed her death. I was unafraid and well supported by the staff. I still remember the lady's name with affection; at least Ada did not die alone.

There was another patient who had been born deaf and dumb and was a good lip reader, who followed me around and began to teach me sign language. When I tried to ask her why she was in the hospital, she always pointed to her throat and ears, indicating her lack of voice and deafness were the only cause of her incarceration. She was so lovely and gentle, and I believe that by her actions she was trying to mother me and keep me safe.

Eventually, I was allowed to leave the ward, and for the first time I could assess where I had been housed. The building reminded me of Rothwell, with its imposing large front door beneath a clock tower. Long cream-tiled corridors seemed to fan out in all directions, at the end of which were more forty-bedded wards similar to the ward where I stayed. A most ornate and, to my mind, beautiful old ballroom graced one corridor. Here, patients gathered each Friday night; many were such good dancers. I could never understand why so many patients appeared so normal but were in this institution. Sadly, some patients wandered aimlessly up and down the corridors and were here evidently for their own protection and care. Many would smile and sing; others looked so lost and forlorn.

I could not have had more freedom had I been handed the keys! As long as I helped around the ward in the morning, I was left to my own devices each afternoon. I was so content with my lot here; no one was hurting me.

I travelled to and from Rothwell and visited my grandmother and other family members. I enjoyed getting to know my true family. However, I discovered that as my brother Stanley was still under the care of the authorities, he could only have restricted visits, and I was barred from visiting his foster home. I had to adhere to the rule not to return to Mario Street, but letters now passed between my dear foster aunts and me. I received my regular letter from the Dean family in Leighton Buzzard, and boxes of flowers once more came my way. I had no choice but to put these in the staffroom – one patient had an appetite for eating flowers!

I had always planned from being a very small child that I wanted to be a nurse. Now I was learning many caring skills and revelled in the need to help others. Not only was I finding that this gave others comfort, it was also satisfying a need within me to be useful and wanted.

However, one day, I got something I didn't want. A fancy-dress party had been arranged between wards. I was padded out with a large bosom and dressed as Ena Sharples, a formidable old character in the early *Coronation Street* series on TV. My hair was covered in flour to change it from auburn to grey and an old grey double-breasted coat and hairnet completed the outfit. I won 200 cigarettes. I didn't smoke, but my prize was soon going up in smoke as patients gathered round for a fag!

★★★

Several attempts by the social workers to transfer me to a Salvation Army hostel and job interviews were arranged. One day, I was taken to a shop selling evening gowns. The owner also made fur coats, and the air was thick with dust. I hated the tiny backroom where I was set to work dusting shelves. One of the other girls working with me also hated the place. We heard that the boss could not stand the sight of blood or descriptions of surgical procedures, so we cooked up some gruesome stories and left with our cards the same day.

I was determined to stay where I was until I was past the age of consent and the committee. I totally refused to leave the place where no one was beating me or making harsh demands on me. It had been almost a year since I had entered the world of the asylum, and I had received nothing but kindness from all the staff. I realise that there were many patients who had not always been shown kindness in this institution, but I can only base these memoirs on the personal care I received. Once again, I had been in the fortunate position when social care of the mentally ill was under much-needed review and considerable changes for the better were being implemented.

One afternoon, I was just about to leave the ward when a message came through from the porter's lodge that I had visitors. I waited in anticipation, only to see two strangers coming through the door. The man was tall with broad shoulders and a rather attractive face. His hair was jet black and just beginning to recede. The woman was small in height, but very plump in body. Her auburn hair was just starting to fade around the edges into a silvery colour which seemed to frame her rounded face. Her toothless smile held my attention for a moment before I turned and walked into the kitchen.

I asked the staff who these people were and was informed that it was my mother and her husband! I was shocked. Over the years, I had imagined what my mother could have looked like. My imaginary impressions were so vastly different from reality.

Several nurses stood in the hall and watched as I tried to come to terms with this awful dilemma. Sadly, I didn't feel any warmth towards the two visitors. I asked how they knew where I was, and was told that my uncle, my mother's brother, had managed to track them down to Bradford. As soon as my mother heard where I was, she had come immediately, even though my uncle wanted to come first and forewarn me.

I heard they had lived in the same house for almost thirteen years. I asked if the social work department knew where they lived. They confirmed they had been to Social Services headquarters at Headingley when I was small. There, they had been assured I lived with a minister and his wife and was settled and very happy. I wondered how many more times I would hear this false statement. It seemed I had not been entirely abandoned. My mother's whereabouts had been known, or easily traceable.

Just when I thought I had heard everything, my mother informed me I had a stepsister, aged nearly thirteen. She was at school, but I could meet her when I went home with them. Home? My home was right here; I had no plans to move to a total stranger's house, even if she was my mother! The visit ended on this note …

The next visitor was Miss Foster. We discussed my future for the first time and it seemed I had little choice in the matter. Only my mother, who had had no input into my life up to now, or a court judge could release me from the hospital. I was classed as not in need of mental health care, a status that I had apparently carried for many months, but now at seventeen, I was still under the age of consent. My mother's sudden appearance was literally letting everyone off the hook regarding my future. During my years in care, I had been aware that some so-called 'lost' parents turned up to reinstate family life once the children were of working age. This looked to me like one such scenario.

The following week, Miss Foster took me to a warehouse in Leeds and purchased a full set of new clothing for me. I was also given a book of saving certificates valued at twenty-one pounds, which Auntie Agnes and Auntie Cissie had been saving until I reached twenty-one years of age. Receiving this gift, I burst into tears and, for the first time, Miss Foster put her arms around me – she too wept.

We went to a nice Chinese restaurant in the centre of Leeds. Enjoying a last meal together, I realised for the first time what a most attractive face Miss Foster had. In fact, she was quite beautiful when she smiled. At last, I was old enough to see not just another irksome social worker with her lists of dos and don'ts, committees and consents. Here was a person going about her daily tasks under the strict confines of a system that was answerable, not only to any parents or to relatives who may pop up at any time unannounced, but also to society who made such high demands, often with no knowledge of child welfare problems and constraints. Throughout the meal I was constantly asked if 'they', Social Services, had always been kind to me. But did 'they' want the whole truth? I said, 'Yes', knowing that most of them had been kind – some had been exceptionally kind … others I should forget!

Miss Foster walked with me to Leeds Station. We embraced as we parted for the last time. Her task had not been easy. Deep down, I liked her better now than I had ever done in the past. I stopped to buy *The Yorkshire Post* at the newspaper stand, which had now moved under cover by the Queens Hotel in City Square. Stanley, the paper seller, still wore the same two old coats, one on top of the other. He still looked so dishevelled and cold.

I boarded a train to Harrogate. Leaving the station there, I felt the warmth of the sun shining on my back. I meandered alone through the town and the beautiful Valley Gardens and enjoyed the complete freedom from hospital life for a few hours. Wandering there amongst the beautiful floral displays, I looked back and reflected on a childhood that had disappeared beneath a pile of consent forms and letters, hidden truths and sometimes blatant lies.

I had known only three people in the system who had abused me, thereby abusing their positions of trust. I had come through some harrowing events which had given me insight into human nature in the raw. I had also had the good fortune to know some extraordinarily kind-hearted people who, despite all my faults and failings, loved me as a person.

My childhood was over. There was no doubt I had matured. I knew I had been richly blessed by many loving, caring, gentle and, above all, honest people, whose only concern was how to support me through the maze of legislation, which blocked their freedom of speech and robbed me of my identity.

Twenty Five

A STRANGE WORLD

Life under my mother's roof in Bradford was so different from anything I had ever encountered. There was no level of hygiene. My stepfather and mother lay in bed most of the morning. As the double bed was next to the front door, I had to pass it each time I left the house. In the mornings, the light disturbed both sleepers, so I learnt to grope my way around the room in the dark. It did save putting another shilling in the meter!

Any attempts by me to clean up the awful mess were thwarted by my stepfather, who thought everyone should sit in front of him and listen to his fanciful tales of a life that bore no reality to my mother's accounts of life after our births, and certainly did not correspond with Social Services documentation. There were times when he would send my mother upstairs in the middle of the night to get me up because he wanted to talk rubbish to me. I conceded to this a few nights, but then, when I was utterly exhausted by broken nights' sleep, I told him 'to get lost' in no uncertain terms.

He would not allow curtains to be opened, and hence we lived in a dark, damp and extremely depressing environment. My mother's only escape was, believe it or not, cleaning other people's houses. I soon discovered she excelled in this and had developed a good clientele who sought her out for their domestic needs. However, her meagre wages and additional benefits barely covered the household outlay.

My two foster aunts' gift of National Saving Certificates settled an outstanding debt at the local shop. This greatly saddened me. I knew how every penny counted for them, and these savings would have been at their own expense and saved over a number of years.

I found work in a bakery about three miles from the house. I walked there and back each day until the shoes I had been provided with by Social Services were worn through. Saturdays were spent trawling the jumble sales where, surprisingly, I found two pairs of shoes in good condition in my size. My stepsister was clothed in the same way.

I was constantly grumbled at if I tried to wash my clothes, and resorted to arriving at work early and washing items out in the ladies' toilets. I then took them home and tried to dry them in my tiny bedroom. This practice didn't last too long. Clothes in a house with no heating upstairs didn't dry in time; woollen items hardly ever dried at all.

One day, the boss at the bakery called me in to the office. He offered me a seat and cup of coffee, before telling me he was concerned for my welfare. Desperately trying to hold back the tears, I explained to him my circumstances. He listened in silence and then said he would see how he could help. Later that day, Edgar called me back to his office. He told me there was a washroom at the back of the bakery; no other staff used this area. His wife provided me with an iron and ironing board. In return, I ironed the cotton jackets used in the bakery and some white aprons. Now, I was able to keep myself clean without all the arguments in the home. I was most grateful to Edgar and his wife for their kindness.

My stepsister was a lovely child. We got on well together, but she faced a lot of bullying at school, especially as she tried to explain this sudden appearance of an older sister. She was artistically very clever. I was able to pass on to her some sewing and knitting skills, but jumble sales did not provide new materials and wool, so irregular availability left some craft work unfinished. To me, her life seemed so restrictive, but then this was the only home she had ever known, whereas I had seen much more of life.

On Sunday mornings, the sound of the Salvation Army Band marching past the house was a reminder of happier days. If I looked out of my tiny bedroom window, I could just see the top of the flag with its crest on the flagpole. I knew the words around it were 'Blood and Fire', meaning the blood of Christ and the fire of the Holy Spirit. How I clung to the Christian teachings of childhood in these dark days. I did pray for my family and my foster aunts and Uncle William. I thought of them daily.

I was denied access to anyone I had known in the past by my mother and stepfather's written conditions laid down on my discharge, stating that all childhood ties were to be severed. Family life was exceptionally strained. We were all strangers to each other's lifestyles, let alone each other's idiosyncrasies. Why my mother stayed in these conditions, I'll never know. She certainly could have lived a more normal life.

Just before my twenty-first birthday, I put into action a plan to get a flat of my own. In fairness to my mother, she took me to some letting agents and showed me the ropes of renting. A flat was available only a short walk away from the bakery. My mother gave me a bed and bedding, some crockery and ten shillings from my last pay packet. I moved out of her house and started life on my own. Surprisingly, my mother never visited my flat after the first day, although we left on speaking terms. I could not reason with this. It was like another rejection.

I heard of a lady in the street who was selling some furniture and arranged with her to pay a weekly amount. Within this first week, I had partly furnished a room, albeit on tick, which I had always been taught to avoid. I settled in full by the given date, and the lady rewarded me with a gift of a studio couch free of charge. I now washed and ironed my own clothes at home but continued to iron the boss's bakery jackets and the aprons, for which he insisted on paying me, against all my protests.

At times, I did feel very lonely; after all, I had never lived alone before. Other people had always surrounded me. I missed their company. I acquired a budgerigar, called Peter, and when I had no one else to talk to, I would chat away to him. He talked non-stop – he had a good teacher!

The first Sunday away from my mother, I telephoned the minister, Reverend McLean, at Beeston Hill Church. He was delighted to hear from me and arranged to go to my foster aunts' house and tell them I was hoping to meet them soon. He took the number of the telephone box opposite my flat and arranged a time for me to return and await a call.

'Praise God! I have prayed this day would come,' said Auntie Agnes. I heard her sobbing down the phone. On hearing her voice again, I too had many tears to wipe away. I wanted to go straight to her, but I had work to do and rent to pay, so I waited until the following Saturday.

The reunion was so joyous it is hard to put into words, except to say that I had truly returned home to two people who were very special and so motherly towards me. Auntie Cissie arrived back from visiting a needy family. She too cried tears of joy. Auntie Agnes said, 'If we don't all stop crying, there will be too many hankies in the wash, so let's have a cup of tea.'

My two dear aunts now lived in a much bigger house not far from Elland Road football ground and within hearing of cheers when the Leeds United side scored a goal. The house was on the sunny side of the street. It still had no garden, but it boasted a bathroom and indoor toilet up two flights of stairs in the attic. The kettle was boiled on the little gas cooker in a separate kitchen. A new settee had replaced the old horsehair chaise longue.

We sat round a new, tiled fireplace and there was now no black fire range to polish. A friend of the sisters had recently left them a few pounds in her will in appreciation for all the care she had received from them in the form of shopping and hot meals when she was no longer able to cook for herself. This gift had allowed them to have the whole house redecorated. The lovely yellow wallpaper reflected the warm sunshine now streaming through the windows.

Strangely, I missed all the old things in Mario Street. A needy family had been the recipient of my bed after my birth mother's demands that there be no more contact with any foster carers.

Mario Street and its homely dwellings, shops, schools and community buildings with their rich history had been savagely crushed and levelled to the ground. The old gas lamps lay in a mangled heap, no longer casting their comforting glow as darkness fell. I wondered how the old, crippled gas lighter, who regularly doled out sticky toffees to children gathered around the lampposts, would now earn his living. The cobbles and scrubbed flagstones, smoothed by 100 years of trampling feet, were now being collected by reclamation dealers, who were selling them on to create new garden paths.

The whole area was beyond all recognition. Standing there gazing at the empty spaces, I felt so bereft, but took comfort in the fact I had not witnessed the demolition of 45 Mario Street. Reflectively, I wandered along Hunslet Hall Road, which crossed between Hunslet and Holbeck. The shops, where gossiping locals had acted as broadcasters of local news and events, were now silent. The humour, often crude (but never rude if children were present), by the mill workers was confined to memory to be recalled in unfamiliar public houses on new estates.

Everywhere I looked, new houses and roads were under construction. A new modern Salvation Army Hall had been built. The buckets that once stood half-full of water beneath the leaking roof in the old hall were now empty and condemned to the cupboard.

My childhood haunts were fast slipping into the history books of time. Two main buildings still survived: Beeston Hill Baptist Church and Beeston Hill Girls' School. These two venues were within walking distance of my aunts' new address. I visited both, and stood outside each building reflecting on the past ... but this time with a positive outlook to the future.

I returned to the cosy fireside of my aunts' modernised house at Recreation Crescent, Holbeck, and realised how much easier life was for them now. They were living in a good area surrounded by some of their former neighbours, who had resisted all attempts to have them rehoused in the high-rise flats that were springing up in and around Leeds.

I remembered, as a child, every Sunday after the morning church service, Auntie Agnes prepared food for an elderly infirm lady called

Miss Wilson. Agnes would place the hot dishes into her basket and, regardless of weather conditions, she travelled the two miles by tram to deliver the meal. One day, Miss Wilson gave Agnes a beautiful Crown Derby tea service. Now Auntie Agnes insisted I take this set to my flat, along with lots of delicately embroidered table linen. With it came the clear instruction: if you ever marry and have a little girl, pass it on to her.

The following week, I invited Auntie Agnes and one of our former neighbours to my flat in Bradford and I proudly poured tea into the Crown Derby cups. (Auntie Cissie was again out on mercy errands caring for a needy family but promised to come and see my flat as soon as possible.) After tea, I displayed the tea set in a small glass-fronted cabinet I had bought myself. I was so proud of my first home. My décor and standards were in many ways influenced by the good foster homes I had been fortunate to live in.

On my next visit, both aunties were together. We were sitting quietly by the fireside when I sensed something was troubling them. I enquired if all was well. They asked if they could share something with me. Auntie Cissie explained to me that she had attended a funeral at the Salvation Army in Leeds of the paper seller from whom we bought our papers.

Tearfully taking me in her arms, she said, 'Do you know the paper man, Stanley, was your father?'

I could not find words to say. These dear ladies had never told me any lies. I knew they would have carefully checked the facts before telling me such sad news. The last time I had bought a paper was the day I said goodbye to Miss Foster. I felt awful: I had not carried out Auntie Agnes's practice of giving Stanley, my father, coins each time she bought her paper, saying, 'Go and get a warm cup of tea.' I remembered his two coats and cold hands, although my two Aunties had given him gloves many times. I recalled his soft-spoken voice even when he called out the words 'Yorkshire Post!' I remembered how he would sometimes disappear. I would presume he had another paper stand somewhere.

He did have another stand! Mr Purnell had told me about my father's visit to HMP for failing to pay maintenance money for me. As a child,

I had never connected the disappearances of the paper man with the details I heard from my child welfare officer. Why did he not tell me the whole truth? I also heard how my father stayed in sheltered accommodation called Shaftsbury House. This hostel was used as a shelter for the homeless. It was almost opposite my school. I couldn't believe how close I had been to my own father. Every day of the school term, I walked around the side of the building. In fact, I had sat on the wall around the complex on the day of the accident at school.

Looking back now through adult eyes at all these events, I realised the tremendous mental strain faced by all my carers, knowing that every time I visited Leeds city centre there was every opportunity for me to discover my father standing there selling papers. I was amazed and at the same time saddened to think that these two remarkable foster aunts had been forced to keep my father's identity from me. What a terrible burden! They had also, for so many years, provided my father with regular food and endless cups of tea! I heard how members of the Salvation Army had frequently given my father a bed for the night, and his partner accommodation in the female hostel in Leeds.

We finished our tea, and the three of us travelled to the Salvation Army Hall in the centre of Leeds where the funeral had taken place some time ago. I spoke to the Salvation Army officer who had conducted the funeral service, which I heard had been well attended. Apparently, Stanley in life was no stranger to this officer. The Salvation Army had provided him with hot meals and renewed his two coats when needed. I heard how Kevin and I had both been dedicated (christened) into the Salvation Army as babies beneath the flag I was now standing under. My Unseen Guest had certainly been with me a long time!

Only now did I fully understand why permission had to be obtained for me to become a baptised member of Beeston Hill Baptist Church. Perhaps, if I had been told these facts, I would not have rebelled so strongly against Social Services' required consent. They had to obtain my father's consent for me to change denominations. If only I had known the real circumstances, how much better it would have been for all concerned. Hidden facts led to rebellion; the teenage years were full of inquisitiveness and searching.

The truth was very painful for me. I grieved for the paper seller who had so often looked me in the face as, together with Auntie Agnes, I had collected the *Yorkshire Evening Post* before returning home to Mario Street. I thought of the times when we would be sitting by our warm fireside eating hot buttered toast and realised my father would have still been out in the cold. I now realised that, had I not been admitted into the children's home, I too might have been cold and hungry. Had my father acted in kindness by admitting Kevin and me into what he thought would be a safe haven? There were so many unanswered questions in my mind and still no knowledge of my brother. My search would go on.

I tried to apologise for my difficult teenage behaviour but Auntie Agnes took hold of my hand and said, 'There is no need to apologise. You never hurt us, but you always hurt yourself.' My two foster aunts assured me they fully understood my need to find my own identity. Their only regret was the horrendous restrictions that, in their own words, almost amounted to deceit, placed upon them to withhold any information they had been given regarding my family. Both aunties were of the opinion that a child has the right to know as much as possible about the circumstances of their admission into the care system. I certainly believe the younger the child is when these details are given, the easier it is for the child to accept the circumstances. Had I been given the facts, I would not have spent most of my childhood days feeling utterly rejected by my family, and then later by Uncle William and Auntie Marjorie.

Within a few weeks of telling me about my father's identity, Auntie Agnes suffered a massive stroke. She was found sitting on the settee. It was evident that she had been preparing to do her regular Sunday visit to some lonely person. In her shopping bag there was cake and a bunch of flowers, probably purchased from the market the day before. Her intended last action was to take joy and comfort to someone. This was so symbolic of a lady who had dedicated her whole life to the needs of others. Hundreds of people gathered at her funeral, and tributes poured

Me, aged twenty-one, with my dear foster aunt - Agnes Muriel Lowe. A real mother figure, who supported me through my childhood.

in from so many who had had the privilege of knowing dear Agnes Muriel Lowe.

Her death left Auntie Cissie and I devastated. I wondered if the strain of the last weeks had been too great for Auntie Agnes, but Auntie Cissie assured me Agnes had for many years suffered from severe high blood pressure and nosebleeds. This diagnosis had been made when Auntie Agnes had to have a medical examination before she could foster me and had almost prevented Agnes from taking me into her home. Again, the strong bond between us had prevailed. This was a crucial factor in the making of the committee's final decision to allow Agnes to foster me.

I continued to visit Auntie Cissie most weekends for the next four years until she died of cancer. Like Agnes, she too offered kindness and support to so many. I had received such kindness in abundance from both my foster aunts. Despite the severe pain and suffering Cissie endured in her last few days, she was seen giving another patient a drink of tea and shared with them that Jesus her Saviour loved them too. Eleanor (Cissie) Lowe died, like her sister, putting other people's needs before her own.

Both ladies had given me a sure foundation for life. I was now very determined to do my best to honour their love and devotion. I sincerely thank God for their lives and for the Christian teaching I received, not from sermons, although Auntie Cissie's sermons at the Salvation Army services were full of faith and encouragement, but from the daily actions of love and devotion to me and others who came their way. I never once heard them say a wrong thing about anyone, although they had supported many who had fallen by the wayside of life. They were human, not entirely perfect, but they were serving a perfect God, and His light certainly shone through their lives.

It is strange sometimes how things can work out for the best. As a little girl, I overheard Auntie Agnes say to a friend, 'I pray every night I live long enough to see the child grow up and be able to fend for herself.' The friend replied that she hoped God would answer her prayer. Her prayer was answered. I was now making my way in life and I still had dreams to fulfil.

In Memory of Agnes and Cissie Lowe

Angels of Light

Angels of light came from heaven,
Sent by the Maker on high,
Seeing a stranger before them,
Silently they draw nigh;
Wiping the tear that is falling,
Comforting messages bring,
Turning the thoughts of the lonely,
Upward, towards the King.

Angels of Light dispel darkness,
Drive all evils away;
Bind up the wounds of the broken,
Teach the lost souls to pray;
Direct the feet of the wayward,
Speak of the Saviour's love;
Angels of Light show mercy,
Revealing the goodness of God.

Twenty Six

SILVER LININGS

The bakery building was due for demolition, along with much of the surrounding area, and redundancies were unavoidable. I was sorry to say goodbye to my work colleagues. I sadly said farewell to Edward, my boss, and his wife who had so often shown me much kindness. It was now time to move forward with a career. I decided I would accept a friend's offer to store all my belongings in her spare room and close my flat.

A friend introduced me to residential work in an unmarried mother and baby home in London. I loved helping the girls with their babies but found the fostering separation days too stressful. In the few months I worked there, I was deeply saddened by the fact that some young women had been admitted to the home on numerous occasions. I realised there were more factors to consider regarding all these unwanted pregnancies.

Some mothers desperately wanted to keep their babies, but homelessness or other social reasons meant the only option on offer was adoption of the child – or children's homes! Once the babies had been taken away, their mothers would leave the same day. It was a double goodbye to mother and child.

I realised very quickly that I had stepped back into institutional life. I absolutely hated the fact that, as a member of staff, these young mothers waited on me, along with other staff, at mealtimes. I voiced my displeasure and I was considered odd and ungrateful by the staff, who saw this as just a benefit of the business. For me, this was far too institutionalised. I quickly reassessed my hopes of a career in the caring profession. I needed to look beyond my upbringing and find true independence.

Throughout all the changes, I had never lost my Christian belief in God above, although I had often experienced moments when I felt alone. In these moments, I would recall Auntie Agnes's illustration of how to cope in times of loneliness. She would say to me, 'Take an empty chair and place it in front of you. Imagine your dearest friend is sitting there and, in your mind, name anyone you know who has troubles, worries or fears. Speak their names individually and ask God to bless them. Then stand up, put the kettle on, make a cup of tea and count your blessings and you will be surprised how good God is.' There have been moments when the kettle has never been off the boil!

I had expressed an interest in going to the Salvation Army Training College for Officers in London, and went for all the interviews, but the officer interviewing me also knew of my childhood desire to be a nurse. He asked if he could share some of the information he had gleaned from me with Matron Willcocks at Mildmay Mission Hospital in London. A few weeks later, I was asked if I would like to visit the hospital and was advised to take a few days to consider both options. I decided on a nursing career. I applied for a post as an auxiliary, not having the education qualifications needed for nursing. I instantly liked Matron, although I could see she would demand very high standards.

Within weeks, I was an auxiliary on a medical ward. I was so happy and contented. All the skills I had learned in the Leeds Hospital were now being put into practice. The difference this made to my life was incredible. I had a purpose to fulfil each day and a warm comfortable room to return to at night. I worked with some excellent nursing sisters, whose willingness to teach me in those early days would be the foundation of a nursing career.

I completed two Aldermaston correspondence courses, in English and human biology. Having achieved an 'A' Pass in the latter, Matron rewarded me with a night out at the theatre with the companion of my choice.

St Matthew's Hospital and the London Jewish Hospital were also under Matron's control. She discussed with me plans for me to transfer to St Matthew's Hospital and commence my nursing training.

Matron was a staunch Salvationist, but she never forced her beliefs on anyone. She led by good example – and a sharp tongue when the need arose. Her corrections to any stepping out of line were administered behind closed doors and were never held against the offender.

I got a couple of reprimands: one was for not wearing my district nursing hat when out on a call during my training. I was, in Matron's eyes, improperly dressed. Another was for cycling all the way from London to Leighton Buzzard through the night to see the Dean family. Dad Dean was very ill, and I wanted to be with him. The telling off from Matron was due to what she called my lack of notifying her of my planned and arduous journey before embarking on such a ride.

I am sure she would have recommended a better way, but nurses' pay was so low, and I had no financial means of getting there except under my own steam and terribly tired legs. I did not dare tell her I had somehow wandered on to a motorway. A passing lorry driver saw my predicament. He put my bicycle on his lorry and drove me to the right country road to Leighton Buzzard.

The meeting to discuss this matter ended with Matron giving me my fare to return to Dad Dean's bedside. Along with the Dean family, I was able to be with him when he died. I had been so blessed to know this dear old gentleman. He had given me hours of fun and laughter and a better knowledge of gardening, a hobby I still enjoy. All my nursing study books had been paid for by him and even my new bicycle had been his gift to me. I was glad I made the journey; it was worth the telling off!

***

I had some very good friends on the same nursing course. Valerie had a lovely Aberdeen accent and was very proud of her Scottish roots. She also had a remarkably attractive face and figure. Many glances came her way from male patients and porters. Her deep sense of Christianity shone through in her life. She had a wonderful sense of humour, and the patients loved her infectious laughter. Val was always kind and very caring towards me.

Huan arrived from Malaysia, along with other girls from that part of the world. I remember being so impressed with her lovely dark brown eyes, sweet, smiling face and gentle nature. She too had a deep faith in God, and it was a real joy to be in her company.

We all completed and passed our nursing exams, much to Matron Willcock's delight, and so plans were made for all of our class to go on to further training. I thought about midwifery, but realised I was too emotionally distressed when dealing with the death of children during my paediatric training. I decided to specialise in medical, surgical, or acute elderly.

One day, I came off duty and was greeted by Valerie. She wanted to go to a dance in Leicester Square. She had been a hairdresser before entering nursing and quickly arranged my long auburn hair. Together, we arrived outside the dance hall. Here, Valerie stopped and, bowing her head, asked God to bless us both and keep us safe. I prayed, 'Lord send me a husband and make it quick!'

The first man who asked for a dance did not know his left foot from his right, possibly due to his alcohol consumption. I politely refused his second dance. The next dancer literally swept me off my feet. He knew all the fancy footwork, but I didn't, and it was my turn to step on his toes! Standing at the side of the dance floor, taking a break to get my breath back, I was approached by a tall, handsome young man, with a rather gentle Scottish accent. His clothes were of such fine quality. He was so polite, such a perfect gentleman. Gosh, did I know at that moment that I was a woman!

We danced together the whole evening, stopping only for a brief interlude when the Joe Loss Band took a break. My new-found companion bought me a coke at my request. I was amazed he didn't pressurise me into taking a stronger drink. I am not sure if I finished my drink or not. Poor man, he just about managed to tell me his name was Robert and that he was passing through London before going on to Romsey to see his brother.

I was so at ease talking to him, and he was such a good listener! I told Robert I was with Valerie. At the end of the evening, he offered to take Valerie and me back to the hospital. I wished he had offered to walk the three miles instead of getting a taxi, just so I could spend more time with him. Leaving us at the porters' lodge, he kissed me goodnight and apparently walked the whole way back to the hotel where he was staying.

The next day, I was the envy of my friends when a huge bouquet of flowers arrived from Robert. Several phone calls from him were put through to the Nurses' Home. The next day, my first love letter arrived. We arranged to meet again on Saturday on the steps of St Paul's. I had shared my good news with the sister on the ward, and she ensured I was off duty on time.

I was so hungry when Robert took me to the Swiss restaurant (money was scarce and we were often hungry), but I still thought I had to eat quickly and allow others to take my place at the table. How institutionalised I had become over the years!

Leaving the restaurant, we walked together down Fleet Street, onto the Strand and through the streets to St James's Park. On the way, I told Robert I worked these streets and his inquisitive look in return amused me! When I was off duty, I *did* work the streets at night – with the Salvation Army soup runs for the homeless! I knew many of the back streets and a good number of the regular visitors to the soup kitchen.

The next few hours were simply wonderful as we shared our thoughts and feelings. Robert told me how he had come into the dance hall to avoid a heavy rain shower. There were certainly no rain showers now. We were so in love with each other. Robert kissed me and asked me to marry him. I said, 'Yes! What's your second name?' We hugged each other and counted up the hours we had spent together in each other's company or on the telephone and realised we had only been in contact with each other for eleven hours.

The Nurses Christian Fellowship met every Monday evening. Matron Willcocks usually conducted this meeting and I thought I had better call at her office before the gathering and share with her my good news. Matron asked me how long I had known Robert. When I replied only eleven hours, she raised her eyebrows in astonishment and said, 'Have you lost your marbles, girl?' As soon as I introduced her to Robert, she asked if there were more like Robert out there. She certainly knew I lost more than my marbles – I was well and truly in love.

Twenty Seven

WEDDING BELLS

A full descriptive letter was quickly sent off to the Dean family, telling them of my handsome prince charming and his purchase of a beautiful engagement ring. An invitation to visit was returned by the next post and the invitation was extended to my friends, Valerie and Huan.

We were greeted at the front door by all the Dean family, who had gathered to meet Robert. I was so proud to introduce him. Auntie Doris asked, 'Where did you find him? Can you find me one like him?' Having now had two requests from single ladies to find more 'Roberts', I knew I must have done something right.

A wonderful spread of food and a beautifully decorated cake with lovely pink roses had been made for our official engagement party. Auntie Doris knew the story of my stolen birthday cake and had tried here to replicate it. As always, all the Dean family had supported me. I shall always be grateful to them for all their kindness. The joy I experienced was so wonderful, I only wished Auntie Agnes and Auntie Cissie could have been there, but they too might have asked me to find them a 'Robert'. I knew in my heart that Dad Dean would have been delighted I had met such a kind gentleman.

After the party, Robert and I travelled to Scotland to meet his parents. We had agreed we would live in Scotland after our marriage. Robert's parents told me they would do all they could to help us prepare for our new life together, and accommodation in their house was offered until we could secure a place of our own. I explained to Robert and his parents the situation regarding my family and my background history. They assured me they were pleased I was going to be part of their family.

A few weeks later, we travelled to Bradford to see my mother and stepfather, whom I had once again traced. The reception was cold and uninviting and Robert was horrified when he saw the conditions I had once lived in. Getting into the car for the homeward journey, I cried. Robert stopped the car in the next layby and took me into his arms. He said to me, 'It's you I am marrying, not your mother, but I do wish she would put her teeth in. She would be so attractive if she did.' I laughed. Now I knew all would be well between us.

We visited Saffron Walden, where Uncle William and Aunt Marjorie now lived having retired from full-time ministry in Jersey. Here, I received such an affectionate greeting and absolute approval of Robert.

***

The next six months were hectic, preparing for our wedding and I was overwhelmed by all the support and kindness I received from so many sources. The hospital chaplain agreed to marry us at the Leysian Mission Church, just around the corner from the hospital; Matron Willcocks offered us the use of the staff dining room for our reception; the porters offered their cars to use for the bridesmaids and guests. Matron had just bought a new white Morris Marina and offered to take me to church in her car. I certainly knew she would ensure this bride arrived on time!

I asked Valerie, Huan and another friend, Kay, to be my bridesmaids. Auntie Doris had their dresses made and also bought our wedding cake. It was designed with the Scottish thistle and the Yorkshire rose on each side. A former patient offered to pay for my dress, and permission was granted by the Hospital Board for me to accept his gift.

Robert's parents and other family members travelled to London to be with us and, along with 100 guests, helped us to celebrate the day. Several elderly long-term patients came down from the wards for the reception, and for those who could not join us, plates of food were sent to the wards. I cried through most of the day, but they were tears of absolute joy as I realised how many good friends I had. Sadly, Uncle William was ill in hospital and could not attend our wedding. We later visited him and shared the highlights of the day with him before embarking on our honeymoon.

We stayed for three days in London and visited the Tower of London to see the Crown jewels, an ambition of mine since my royal scrapbook days. When we returned to Scotland, a work colleague of Robert's kindly gave us the use of his car so we were able to enjoy trips around the Trossachs and other beauty spots around Perthshire. I had never seen such beautiful hills and mountains, and immediately loved the Scottish landscape. On the rainy days, the rainbows were spectacular.

I was on cloud nine. My entire life had been transformed into something so beautiful. Robert's gentleness and caring support gave me confidence and assurance. I no longer felt alone. I was legally now part of a real family.

★★★

Robert and I returned to Edinburgh and spent the first six months in a flat in Manor Place, at the West End of town. From here, I could walk to the hospital for work. We both accepted any opportunities for overtime until we had secured enough money for a deposit for our own home.

Our first flat in Roslin on the outskirts of Edinburgh was bijou and cosy. I soon realised I had married a real gentleman, whose only concern was to make me happy and help me fulfil my desire to create a warm, loving home.

Aunt Doris from Leighton Buzzard visited Scotland for the first time and stayed with us for a few weeks. I realised how Doris had over the years been a real, sincere friend to me, and now she extended that friendship to Robert, who greatly valued her sincerity and kindness. We were so delighted to be able to show her our lovely surroundings of great beauty and historical interest.

Much of our spare time was spent walking the hills around Edinburgh and Robert arranged outings to many of Scotland's historic sights. One Sunday, we attended the service in the magnificent St Giles Cathedral in the Royal Mile in Edinburgh, followed by lunch at a hotel in the heart of the city.

Life seemed so peaceful now and I no longer lived with fear and uncertainty. Robert's caring nature and acceptance of me as a person with hopes and aspirations helped me to overcome many of the early feelings of rejection. I still harboured a deep desire to find Kevin, although I was now able to see things in a more mature way. I realised that, even if I could find a way of tracing my brother, he had the right to remain anonymous if he so wished, having been legally adopted and thereby taken on a new identity and lifestyle. Despite my yearnings, I reasoned it would be kinder to stand aside and not search for him – but I would never forget him.

Twenty Eight

CIRCLES OF LIFE

A year after our marriage, we were so delighted to tell family and friends that we were expecting our first child. The sewing and knitting skills I had been taught by my foster aunts were used to make baby clothes and cot bedding. Robert's mother and I enjoyed several shopping sprees together buying nursery items. I was fortunate to have such a good mother-in-law and greatly valued her support and guidance.

One day, I was just about to prepare Robert's tea when the telephone rang. The voice on the phone said, 'Hello. It's Kevin here.'

It is a wonder I did not go into labour with the shock! I asked where he was.

'I am just around the corner in the phone box,' he replied.

Within minutes, we were in each other's arms. It was like a dream, except I was fully awake. His deep blue eyes still sparkled. His red hair was thinner than I remembered, but then he had only been a year old when we had been so cruelly separated. When he was four years old, we had been in the same room, but not told we were brother and sister.

There was no doubt we were related – we even looked alike. I was overwhelmed with joy. I could not believe I was holding in my arms the little brother I had cuddled on that awful day when we were admitted into separate children's homes. He was now twenty-seven, a grown man, but still my brother. Despite all my years of searching, I had not found Kevin – he had found me.

Robert arrived home and immediately liked Kevin. Fortunately, I had a chicken roasting in the oven, so there was ample food for all of us. This would be a special meal; the first Kevin and I had shared since the day we had been so hastily parted. The conversation flowed easily as there were so many gaps to fill.

Kevin had remembered his original surname. He had also been told that he had been adopted and he had an older sister. Robert and I laughed when Kevin told us that a visit to the local fish shop gave him the first glimpse of me. His chips were wrapped in a copy of the newspaper carrying the story of my reunion with our stepbrother. Kevin had run home and showed the article to his parents, who confirmed we were all related. I asked why he chose not to meet me straight away. He explained that he felt, for personal reasons, the time was not right for us to be reunited. Aware of the difficulties adoptive children face when confronted by their real histories, I did not pursue this question.

I asked Kevin where he lived now. I was stunned when he told me he lived in Shadwell, only a few miles along the road from Street Lane Reception Centre. His home was also within easy walking distance of Roundhay Park, where I had so often played in childhood. When I heard of Kevin's home address, I realised I had passed his house many times while out walking in the area. No wonder I had been hastily removed to a locked ward in Highroyds. I had been so very close to finding my legally adopted brother, I realised I had become an embarrassment and a liability to the authorities.

The details I had been so belatedly given of his adoption were correct. Kevin's adoptive parents had relatives living in Buckinghamshire. They had chosen to stay there until his adoption process had been finalised, and then they returned to Yorkshire. Kevin had done his own research and, having seen my regular, updated letters held on file at Social Services headquarters, he was able to obtain my address.

I was naturally delighted to be reunited at last with my long-lost brother, but shocked that the authorities had not contacted me to forewarn me of the pending reunion. I was even more shocked when I discovered that Kevin's parents lived not far from my child welfare officer! He had again told them I was happily settled with a minister and his wife.

Kevin had made plans to return on the overnight bus to Leeds, which was scheduled to leave later that evening. It was such a strange feeling standing there, heavily pregnant with our first child, hugging my younger brother, the baby I had hugged so many years ago. My arms were no longer empty. Kevin was now held firmly in them, his blue eyes and mine bathed in tears – tears of unspeakable joy.

We arranged for us to visit Kevin in Leeds once the baby was born. As I was only a few days away from my delivery date, Robert was anxious for me to stay home and rest, so he walked with Kevin back to the bus stop. In the next post, Kevin sent a letter enclosing money for us to buy a pram and other items for the impending birth. He said he was longing to be part of his real family again.

Within days of Kevin's visit, our little son David was born, bringing such joy to everyone. He too had lovely blue eyes and fair hair, which gradually darkened over the next few months. Robert was a doting father. He would arrive home from work and literally take over from me, caring for our dear little boy. We were so blissfully happy. I returned to nursing part time. Between us, we were able to care for David without outside help, due mainly to opposite shift patterns.

***

We visited Kevin's home and received a very warm welcome. It was evident that Kevin had been a much wanted and loved child. His father was of the old disciplinarian school and he had very high expectations of Kevin. His mother was extremely protective, to the point where this had sometimes provoked jealousy and conflict between his parents.

Kevin had a great love for both parents and always expressed his gratitude for their care. I asked Kevin if he ever wondered what his real parents were like. He admitted there were times when he longed to know more about his background but was afraid to ask in case it upset his adoptive parents. I fully understood this dilemma. This is a common situation children face when separated from their birth parents and attached to new families.

Over the next few months, Kevin and I corresponded by letter and telephone. Kevin shared with me his memories of the last year spent in Rachael Nursery, where he had lived until the age of four. He had two very vivid memories of beatings and abuse, which occurred just before his adoption. He spoke of the deep loneliness he had experienced. He said it was so helpful to talk to someone who really understood the extreme loneliness children in care feel, even when crowds of other children and a few adults surround them. When Kevin heard the truth that our birth mother had abandoned us, he acknowledged he was fortunate to have been legally adopted.

During these conversations, I became very aware that all was not well for Kevin; the early parental separation had taken its toll on such a young life. He suffered from bouts of deep depression and lack of self-worth. There is no doubt Kevin underestimated his own abilities. He had attended Leeds College and was voted top student of the year for his carpentry skills.

He was also an accomplished violinist and had a very good singing voice. Kevin said he would teach me to sing. He hastily changed his mind when he discovered his sister was tone deaf!

Over the next two years, Robert and I made numerous visits to Leeds, as well as to Leighton Buzzard, where the Dean family adored David. We also travelled to London to see Matron Willcocks and my other nursing friends. Everywhere, we shared our joy with people who, in their own way, had brought such contentment into our lives.

We had planned to spend David's second Christmas visiting friends and then stop on the way home at Shadwell. On our arrival, we discovered that Kevin was now very rarely allowed in the home of his adoptive parents due to recent friction between him and his father. He had moved into his own flat.

A concession had been made for him to meet us at his parents' home. We sensed the tension and were so sorry we had not known of these matters before our visit. Kevin immersed himself in feeding and amusing David. He certainly loved our little boy. A date was set for him to come to our home in Scotland for a holiday. As we bid each other farewell, Kevin held me in his arms and said to me, 'Look after David.' I assured him I would always care for him.

By the time we arrived in Roslin, it was nearly midnight. We had attended to David's needs on the journey, and so I laid him in his cot as soon as we entered the house. Exhausted by the long journey, I too went to bed, and Robert made us both a drink before retiring himself.

Just then, the telephone rang. We were shocked to hear that Kevin was in intensive care following a massive overdose of tablets. Despite the long car journey we had just made, Robert reloaded the car and made a bed on the back seat for David.

We travelled for most of the long, sad journey back to Leeds in silent disbelief, arriving at the hospital just before daybreak. Kevin was on a ventilator. His young athletic body now lay so still and his blue eyes were closed. I knew from my nursing knowledge that I would never again see them open.

I took his hand in mine and felt the clammy sweat dampen the palm of my hand. Seeing Kevin lying there, I knew there was little hope of a full recovery and sitting by Kevin's bed, lovingly supported by Robert, I felt as though a wonderful dream had turned into a horrible nightmare.

The doctors were carefully monitoring the situation. I knew in my heart that they would have tried desperately to restore life to Kevin, but there is limited medical treatment available in the event of large amounts of barbiturate poisoning. There was confusion as to who was Kevin's next of kin. His adoptive parents put the decision-making on my shoulders, saying I was Kevin's legal next of kin. (I learned later that this was not entirely so, as Kevin had been legally adopted.)

In moments like these, reality and facts can be blurred. I fully understood how they could be confused with the legalities of next of kin. I was the blood relative of Kevin, but our birth rights had been lawfully changed. I telephoned my friend and advisor, Matron Willcocks, who offered the verbal support I needed from the medical point of view.

The ventilator, which kept Kevin alive for the next two weeks, was eventually turned off. Kevin died without ever regaining consciousness.

At his funeral, large crowds gathered. The child who had been adopted into the community had grown into a much-loved and respected member of society.

Dark clouds had certainly come over us. I had to cope with real surges of anger, frustration and a sense of blame. I thought of the insensitivity of those who had separated brother and sister, leaving each with long years of uncertainty and the trauma of an adult reunion. I struggled with my Christian beliefs, accepting that my prayers to see Kevin again had been answered – but why this sudden and most tragic separation?

For weeks, I could find no answer or inner pacification. Then one night, the answer came to me – God was not to blame. As children, we had no choice in the decision to be placed in the care system. As adults, the role had changed, and our choice had been to be reunited. Now, for reasons I will never be able to explain, Kevin had chosen suicide. Having known such dark hours in my teenage years, when I wanted to leave behind the despair and loneliness I felt at the time, I was so aware of the darkness Kevin must have been passing through to come to such a drastic decision.

One of my greatest dilemmas was whether I should try to contact my mother and tell her about Kevin. Although we had sent my mother and stepfather invitations to our wedding, we had not received a reply. They had literally disappeared again. I eventually came to the conclusion that this action would be inappropriate, in view of the fact that Kevin had been legally adopted. His parents had rights of respect, having dedicated their lives to caring for my brother.

Robert and his family were kind to me as they tried to comfort me, and friends and nursing colleagues all offered their care and support. A few months after Kevin's funeral, I plucked up the courage to revisit Leeds and stayed with Kevin's adoptive parents again. Their lives had also been shattered; they too had had dreams, aspirations, and the possibility of future grandchildren. I heard many things about my brother's life. He had always hoped he would one day find and marry the right girl. Apparently, he longed to have what he called his own family. Kevin and I had shared the same need to find our identities.

Our little two-year-old son was, for us, the only ray of light. David loved toys he could dismantle and rebuild. He was showing a liking for mechanical things, especially his father's first train set, which I had bought Robert for our first wedding anniversary. We had, at the time, an old clock on which David loved to turn the handles around. One day, I was sitting crying over Kevin's death when our dear little son came with his broken clock. Placing the clock in my hands, he cuddled me and said, 'This to make mummy better.' I was so moved by this little act of kindness that I later wrote the following poem.

David's Time

A clock you gave me as a gift,
Two little eyes you did lift.
The clock had seen a brighter day,
No longer ticking time away.
In that little act so kind
I felt such love and peace of mind,
A second at a time should be,
A second not eternity …
As I gazed into your eyes,
Suddenly the darker skies
Became a lighter hue.
Little boy, if you but knew,
Your act turned dark clouds into blue.

I realised that the handles on a clock could be turned back manually, but real time stays in the present. I knew I had a tremendous responsibility to care for our little boy. Life had to go on. Kevin would want the best for his much-loved little nephew, and I, as a mother, had a duty of care along with Robert to ensure David had the best thing we could ever give him – love in abundance.

A year later, we were blessed by the birth of our daughter, Moira. She was such a quiet baby with a captivating smile. She certainly had her father wrapped around her little finger! Her love of animals was evident from an early age; she even dressed our first collie dog, Lassie, in her old clothes because she didn't want her to catch cold. The joys these two little ones bought into our life were immeasurable.

Robert's parents were extremely kind to the children and a tremendous support to us. We felt so blessed. There was now barely any time for Auntie Agnes's empty chair strategy, and cups of tea often went cold, but there were so many blessings to count.

Twenty Nine

PANDORA'S BOX

Realising that Kevin had obtained my details via Social Services records, I decided I would contact them with a view to seeing all the information on my file. Incredibly, the file was intact (many files were destroyed, leaving children without a means of searching for their identity).

Throughout my childhood, I had been repeatedly denied information regarding the circumstances surrounding my admission into the children's homes. Now the facts were laid bare, and I was horrified by the information gleaned.

There, on file, was a letter written in my own father's handwriting, stating clearly that Kevin and I were not to be separated. There was evidence that my father had been hounded from one town to the next by a male social worker who constantly put pressure upon him to sign Kevin over for adoption. My father's poor financial situation and failure to pay our maintenance costs had been used as a bargaining tool until he finally relented and signed the adoption papers. Now I have these documents as evidence.

So, my father did care what became of Kevin and me, but poverty had driven him to have us admitted to care. We were voluntary admitted under Section 1, and he had tried desperately to keep us together. The system failed him, and Kevin and I were separated. The system had certainly failed to respect our human rights.

Now, with my hands firmly clutching a letter in Auntie Marjorie's handwriting, I closed my eyes and asked God's forgiveness for ever doubting these two people who had longed to take me as their own child. The letter outlined so clearly their desire to continue seeing me and even requested that I be transferred to another home, nearer their new manse in Cheltenham so they could maintain their friendship. Every letter highlighted their love for me. How terribly sad it must have been for them to receive so many refusals to continue seeing me. I can find no reason on file for them to be denied contact with me, but all requests were rigorously denied by the committee, as copies of their letters now reveal.

Auntie Marjorie and Uncle William would have been absolutely devastated if they had known the trauma of that farewell. Now, I understood why my little dress had hung for so many years in their wardrobe; they had hoped their contact would be quickly renewed. Reading these letters relieved so much hidden tension. Nothing can destroy a child's confidence more than deceitfulness, and this came in the form of silence.

Did the committee members (many of whom I never met) fail to consider the impact their decision making would have in the long term? Had I known these facts at a young age, I would have been able to grow in the knowledge that I was not 'A Nobody's Child' left firstly by my mother and my father. The minister and his wife came forward with the view to adopt a child. I was chosen, and they soon genuinely loved me, and I adored them, but their circumstances had changed. I can only speculate that perhaps my father or Leeds Social Services did not want me moved from the area. As a five-year-old, I was considered capable of scrubbing floors, or serving staff their meals, but not capable of being consulted about my feelings regarding my love for my foster aunt and uncle. Neither was I asked if I still wanted to have contact with them after their transfer to another church.

My very own loving family. Husband Robert, daughter Moira, son David and grandson Jamie.

It is amazing that, as an adult, I can see so many facets to my case with arguments for and against issues surrounding my life. Indeed, this makes me reflect on the present roll of all social workers who have so many complex and difficult cases still within the care system.

Much has changed for the better since the years I spent in children's homes and I was so fortunate to be in the early stages of some of those changes. I hold up Ann Smith's home as the finest example of a family-orientated home where siblings stayed together. If circumstances prevent brothers and sisters staying under one roof, they at least have the right to know of each other's existence and have as much contact as possible.

I sincerely marvel at how so many broken circles have been joined together again by My Unseen Guest, my childhood name for Jesus. I thank those who genuinely cared for me throughout my childhood years. Our friends and families were able to watch David and Moira develop into young people. They knew Auntie Doris in Leighton Buzzard as Nana – what an excellent influence she was on their young lives! Both children loved her and always looked forward to our visits to Leighton Buzzard.

I have happy memories of when my brother and I walked with his little nephew through the lanes we both knew so well. I am sure he would have taken his niece down the same lanes in Shadwell, or perhaps to Roundhay Park, just along the road.

Above all, I look back with deep gratitude and thank God for my two dear foster carers. Age proved to be no barrier to the immeasurable love and devotion I was shown by Agnes Muriel and Eleanor 'Cissie' Lowe. Love does not have an age, but it has endurance if it sustains another human being. Their love sustained me in times of need.

Finally, I thank my dear husband Robert, for all the years he has lovingly supported me, through various trials and difficulties. We have also shared times of great joy and happiness, strengthening our deep love for each other. Our children, David and Moira, gave us the longed-for family lives we both desired, and will always remain our pride and joy.

I rejoice in the knowledge that, together, Robert and I were able to meet my little brother, Kevin.

G.J. Urquhart

Memorandum

Sadly, after forty-two happy years together, my darling husband Robert died before the publication of these memoirs. It was Robert who encouraged me to write my story, in the hope that it would help to heal many childhood scars. It was with his love and support that I was able to eventually accept I was NOT a nobody's child! This kind and loving gentleman left our family a legacy of love, not a burden of tears.

Acknowledgements

I'm deeply grateful to Robert, David and Moira for their loving support in writing these memoirs. My sincere gratitude to the Reverend Dr Ian Thomson and his wife, Morag, for their patience, wisdom and encouragement. My appreciation to Peter Higginbotham, for introducing me to The History Press and his willingness to provide the foreword. Finally, thank you to the editorial staff and publishers at The History Press, for allowing my story to be told.